Data Visualization

FOR

DUMMIES®

A Wiley Brand

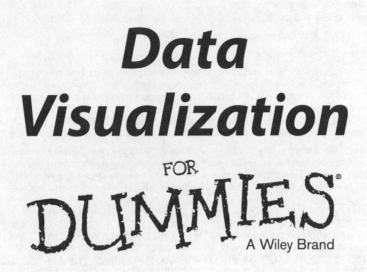

Data Visualization

FOR DUMMIES®

A Wiley Brand

by Mico Yuk
Stephanie Diamond

Data Visualization For Dummies®

Published by: **John Wiley & Sons, Inc.,** 111 River Street, Hoboken, NJ 07030-5774, www.wiley.com

MARCH 2014

Contents at a Glance

Introduction 1

Part I: Getting Started with Data Visualization 5

Chapter 1: Introducing Data Visualization..7
Chapter 2: Exploring Common Types of Data Visualizations 13
Chapter 3: Knowing What You Must about Big Data..................................29

Part II: Mastering Basic Data Visualization Concepts ... 39

Chapter 4: Using Charts Effectively..41
Chapter 5: Adding a Little Context 53
Chapter 6: Paying Attention to Detail..67

Part III: Building Your First Data Visualization 79

Chapter 7: Defining an Easy-to-Follow Storyboard......................................81
Chapter 8: Developing a Clear Mock-Up 99
Chapter 9: Adding Effective Visuals to Your Mock-Up.............................109
Chapter 10: Adding Functionality and Applying Color 131
Chapter 11: Adding Some Finishing Touches...147
Chapter 12: Exploring User Adoption 161

Part IV: Putting Data Viz Techniques into Practice 169

Chapter 13: Evaluating Real Data Visualizations 171
Chapter 14: Recognizing Newbie Pitfalls 191

Part V: The Part of Tens 207

Chapter 15: Top Ten Data Visualization Resources....................................209
Chapter 16: Top Ten Fears of New Data-Viz Creators................................213

Index.. 219

Table of Contents

Introduction *1*

Part I: Getting Started with Data Visualization *5*

Chapter 1: Introducing Data Visualization 7
Understanding Data Visualization 7
  Understanding the importance of data viz 8
  Discovering who uses data viz 8
Recognizing the Traits of Good Data Viz 9
Embracing the Design Process 9
Ensuring Excellence in Your Data Visualization 10

Chapter 2: Exploring Common Types of Data Visualizations 13
Understanding the Difference between Data Visualization
  and Infographics 13
Picking the Right Content Type 16
Appreciating Interactive Data Visualizations 18
Observing Visualizations in Different Fields 19
Using Dashboards 22
Discovering Infographics 22
  Examining different types of infographics 23
  Taking advantage of online infographic tools 26

Chapter 3: Knowing What You Must about Big Data 29
Defining Big Data 29
Seeing How Big Data Changes Business 30
  Getting to know your customers 31
  Discovering the Four V's 32
  Collecting structured and unstructured data 33
  Ensuring the use of quality data 34
Avoiding Dying by Tool Choice 35
  Tableau 36

Part II: Mastering Basic Data Visualization Concepts.... 39

Chapter 4: Using Charts Effectively..............................41
Deciding Which Charts to Use and When to Use Them 41
    Understanding where newbies should start 42
    Choosing simple and effective charts 43
    Using gauges and scorecards to monitor 47
    Finding online tools for chart making 49
Dipping Into Less-Common Charts 49

Chapter 5: Adding a Little Context..............................53
Making Text Useful 55
    Adding text labeling 56
    Considering text positioning 57
    Choosing text fonts 58
    Choosing text color 60
Exploring Text Analysis 61
    Determining what makes text analysis so important 63
    Building a text analysis statement 63

Chapter 6: Paying Attention to Detail..........................67
Uncovering How People Digest Data.. 67
Presenting Common Visual Patterns 71
    Z and F patterns 72
    Pattern design 73
Deciding to Use a Template 74
Achieving Consistency across Devices.. 75
    Embracing responsive design 76
    Following app design standards 77

Part III: Building Your First Data Visualization.............. 79

Chapter 7: Defining an Easy-to-Follow Storyboard 81
Business Intelligence Overview 82
Delving Into Your Story 83
    Uncovering storyboard content.. 84
    Identifying your audience 85
    Documenting Goals.. 87
    Documenting KPIs.. 89
Building Your First Storyboard... 91
    Section 1: Current State 91
    Section 2: Trends 92
    Section 3: Forecast.. 94
    Section 4: What-if 95

Chapter 8: Developing a Clear Mock-Up **99**

Getting Started with Your Mock-Up 100
    Sticking to black and white 100
    Using good ol' pencil and paper 101
    Using web-based or desktop tools 103
Building Template Layouts 105

Chapter 9: Adding Effective Visuals to Your Mock-Up **109**

Recognize the Three Traits of an Effective Visual 110
    Data is clear 110
    Visual fits the data 112
    Exceptions are easy to spot 112
Focus on Insight, Not Hindsight 113
Add Visuals to Your Mock-Up 114
    Section 1: Current State 115
    Section 2: Trends 118
    Section 3: Forecast 125
    Section 4: What-If 127

Chapter 10: Adding Functionality and Applying Color **131**

Recognizing the Human Components 131
    Humanizing your visualizations 132
    Thinking mobile first 132
    Adding functionality 133
    Choosing navigation by using rules 134
    Identifying the most popular menu types 136
Dipping Into Color 139
    Taking advantage of company branding guidelines 139
    Choosing colors without guidelines 142
    Using RAG colors 144

Chapter 11: Adding Some Finishing Touches **147**

Choosing Useful Links 147
    Introducing six mandatory links 149
    Including a last updated timestamp 154
Adding Legal Stuff 155
    Embracing the copyright 155
    Delving into terms and conditions 156
Discovering Visual Cues 156
Adding Location Intelligence 158

Chapter 12: Exploring User Adoption **161**

    Understanding User Adoption 162
    Considering Five UA Measurements 162
    Marketing to Data Viz Users 163
        Ensure data availability and accuracy 164
        Use buy-in and ownership to engage users 164
        Give each data viz the right name 164
        Use internal social media platforms and intranets 165
        Go live on internal platforms 166
        Do away with training 166
        Make sure that the data viz looks great 166
        Provide 24/7 accessibility 166
        Provide speed and reliability 166
        Speed the delivery of your data viz 167

Part IV: Putting Data Viz Techniques into Practice 169

Chapter 13: Evaluating Real Data Visualizations **171**

    Analyzing Data Visualizations by Category 171
        Big-picture considerations 172
        Color 173
        Design issues 173
        Text formatting 174
        Menus 175
        Interactivity 175
        Design for mobile 175
    Evaluating Data Visualizations 176
        Data visualization 1 176
        Data visualization 2 177
        Data visualization 3 178
        Data visualization 4 180
        Data visualization 5 181
        Data visualization 6 182
        Data visualization 7 183
        Data visualization 8 185
        Data visualization 9 186
        Data visualization 10 187
        Data visualization 11 188
        Data visualization 12 189

Chapter 14: Recognizing Newbie Pitfalls 191

Going Overboard with Data...192
Falling into the One-Shoe-Fits-All Trap 193
Focusing on the Tool Instead of the Story 194
Building Mobile Last...195
Abusing Pie Charts 197
Using Green for Alerts...197
Ignoring Basic Statistics...200
    Knowing the probability that an event will occur 200
    Applying variance to show the magnitude of change.......201
    Forecasting the future...202
Not Mastering User Engagement 204

Part V: The Part of Tens 207

Chapter 15: Top Ten Data Visualization Resources 209

Edward Tufte...209
Visual.ly 210
The Functional Art...210
Visualizing Data 210
Chart Porn 210
The Excel Charts Blog...211
FlowingData...211
Datavisualization.ch..211
GE Data Visualization 211
#dataviz and #bigdata...212

Chapter 16: Top Ten Fears of New Data-Viz Creators 213

Telling the Wrong Story...213
Creating an Ugly Data Viz 214
Picking the Wrong Things to Measure.................................214
Alienating Other Stakeholders..215
Misunderstanding the Audience for Your Data Viz..............215
Forgetting about Copyrights and Legal Matters..................216
Selecting the Wrong Tool 216
Making the Wrong Chart Choices..217
Picking Bad/Noncomplementary Colors 217
Using Too Much Data...218

Index 219

Introduction

Data visualization (also known as *data viz*) is a hot topic. With the development of more data sources, such as social media platforms, photos, and customer reviews, Big Data has become a concern for small businesses and large corporations alike. Data is coming from all parts of the business like finance, customer service, and sales, and using it effectively helps you gain a competitive advantage.

It's no longer sufficient to use a multiple-page spreadsheet to present findings about your data. You need to tell visual data stories that produce important insights. This book shows you some ways to create and display data visualizations, including infographics, dashboards, and business intelligence (BI) graphics.

Many experts in the field have created inspiring data visualizations that dazzle the eye. You should be inspired by them, rather than humbled. Not every data viz can — or should — be a devastating work of art. Some visualizations just need to get the job done. But you do want to give yourself every opportunity to create something special. We believe that reading this book will put you on the right path.

About This Book

This book was written to provide you all the information you need to get started creating high-value data visualizations. Use it as a reference guide when you're trying to select the right data, charts, text, and menus to add to your creations.

Data visualizations can be visually creative, such as infographics, or straightforward, such as dashboards. The key to creating the right one for you is to follow the Business Intelligence Dashboard Formula (BIDF), outlined in Part III of this book, and apply it to the different types of visualizations you need to create. It is suggested that you go through Part III in the order in which it is written so that you can follow the progression of the data viz from start to finish.

Within this book, you may note that some web addresses break across two lines of text. If you're reading this book in print and want to visit one of these web pages, simply key in the web address exactly as it's noted in the text, pretending that the line break doesn't exist. If you're reading this as an e-book, you've got it easy; just click the web address to be taken directly to the web page.

Foolish Assumptions

We assume that you're a highly intelligent person who is both creative and business-minded, with a flair for presenting visually appealing graphics — you wouldn't be reading this book if you weren't, right? — but you may be making your first foray into the world of data viz. So we also assume that you're reading this book for any of the following reasons:

- You want to demonstrate to your colleagues that you can make data more useful by displaying it visually.
- You need to gain more direct knowledge about how your customers feel about your products.
- You're tired of using a spreadsheet program to create all your data visualizations and want to try other techniques.
- Your manager wants to use BI dashboards, and you've been chosen to make that happen.
- You want to provide your customers with useful data visualizations that help raise your company's visibility when it is shared by others.

Icons Used in This Book

We packed this book with all sorts of tips, warnings, and other good hints so that you can benefit from our experience. They're identified by the following icons:

This icon lets you know about a way to make things easier, faster, or just plain smarter. Who doesn't want to be smarter?

This icon calls out something you need to remember, so take note. You may even want to write down the information.

We don't want to scare you, but we certainly want to warn you about things to avoid at all costs. Take heed.

This icon points out things that are more technical in nature. If geekiness isn't your thing, don't worry; the technical information is here for your edification if you want it.

Beyond the Book

We wrote extra content that you won't find in this book. Visit www.dummies.com/extras/datavisualization to find the following:

- ✏ A handy list of "Ten Unbreakable Rules for Using Text in a Data Visualization"

- ✏ Additional information on using the Business Intelligence Dashboard Formula (BIDF) Blueprint

- ✏ A downloadable worksheet to help you determine what to include in your data viz

- ✏ A Part of Tens called "Top Ten Blunders to Avoid When Creating a Data Visualization"

Where to Go from Here

You can travel at least two paths when reading this book: You can start at the beginning and wend your way around the topics to familiarize yourself with each one, or you can skip right to the juicy parts that interest you. It's up to you. Either way, we want you to feel confident that you've chosen the right path for yourself. We hope that this book will get you where you want to go. Enjoy the journey!

Part I
Getting Started with Data Visualization

In this part . . .

- ✔ Find out why data viz is important, who uses it, and how the design process affects the creation of a data viz.

- ✔ Recognize the traits of a good data viz and become familiar with the common types of data visualizations.

- ✔ Understand Big Data and find out how to identify and use structured and unstructured data.

Introducing Data Visualization

In This Chapter

▶ Delving into data visualization

▶ Deploying data visualizations for your audience

▶ Embracing the data visualization design process

*I*f you're reading this book, you're probably interested in finding better ways to visualize your information. When you help people visualize the meaning of data, you add tremendous value to any organization. In this chapter, we look at what data visualization is and what it means to different groups.

When it comes to gaining valuable insight in a company setting, the use of data visualization is critical. Companies are desperate to view and learn from their Big Data. Data visualization, however, is a growing field with a critical shortage of true experts.

Big Data refers to the voluminous amounts of information that can be collected from social media data as well as internal company data. Analyzing and extracting insights from it is the goal.

After reading this book, you'll be able to help fill that role for your company, whether you're building your first data visualization or your hundredth one.

Understanding Data Visualization

Here's a simple definition of data visualization: It's the study of how to represent data by using a visual or artistic approach rather than the traditional reporting method.

Two of the most popular types of data visualizations are dashboards and infographics, both of which use a combination of charts, text, and images to communicate the message of the data. The practice of transforming data into meaningful and useful information via some form of visualization or report is called Business Intelligence (BI).

Understanding the importance of data viz

Data visualizations (you can call them *data viz* for short) are widely used in companies of all sizes to communicate their data stories. This practice, known as BI, is a multibillion-dollar industry. It continues to grow exponentially as more companies seek ways to use their big data to gain valuable insight into past, current, and future events.

With the recent popularity of social media and mobile apps, the amount of data that's generated on a moment-to-moment basis is astounding. For this reason, many companies find that making sense of that data requires the use of some form of data visualization. It's virtually impossible to view 1 million rows of data and try to make sense of it!

Imagine going out to your garage every morning, jumping into your car, and then heading to work blindfolded. Chances are that you wouldn't make it past the driveway without having an accident. The same is true for a company that lacks insight into what its data is telling it. This lack of insight is dangerous, and its ramifications could be quite costly, both short- and long-term. Therefore, it's critical that companies use their data to gain insights about their performance.

This book focuses specifically on data visualizations that contain intelligent data (data that is actionable) and that provide some value to a company by enabling a person or group of people to make faster decisions based on that data.

Discovering who uses data viz

Data visualizations are for everybody. All of us use them, whether or not we realize it. If you use apps on your smartphone, for example, chances are that you depend on data visualizations to make critical decisions on an almost daily basis. Do you ever use a weather app to determine how to dress for that day? If you open the app and see a cloud with lightning at the top of the app, you have a good idea that it's going to be a stormy, rainy day without having to read any data about temperature, barometric pressure, and humidity.

This example shows you how a simple visual helps you gain quick insight and make a quick decision (in this case, to wear a raincoat and carry an umbrella). Believe it or not, you just consumed a good data visualization!

Recognizing the Traits of Good Data Viz

Good data visualizations come in all shapes and sizes, but all of them have certain traits, which we discuss in this section.

Mico once worked with a talented graphic-design expert named Natasha Lloyd to deliver a well-received presentation called "How to Build a Successful Business Intelligence Dashboard" at a major global conference. When she was asked what she thought was important about creating visualizations, Natasha said her focus wasn't on what was pretty versus ugly; her focus was on the end-user experience. Table 1-1 shows the key items discussed during the presentation.

Table 1-1	Traits of a Good Data Visualization
Trait	*Description*
Useful	People use it on a regular basis and can make relevant decisions by viewing all the information they need in one place.
Desirable	It's not only easy to use but also pleasurable to use.
Usable	People who use it can accomplish their goals quickly and easily.

Although these traits sound more like descriptions of a new car than descriptions of business data, focusing on these three traits for all your data visualizations should ensure that you produce something that's not only great to look at but that also provides value and deep insight to those who use it.

Although the information in Table 1-1 may seem to be simple, we advise you to use it the way we do: as a tool to measure every data viz against, to ensure that you're focusing on the most important items. Your main goal should be to develop a data visualization that provides key insights to its users.

Embracing the Design Process

One of the main goals of this book is to guide you through the process of scoping, designing, and building your first data viz utilizing intelligence data.

Many methodologies and best practices are available in the marketplace. The ones described in this book are based on Mico's experience in building more than 400 enterprise-grade intelligent data visualizations, first as a consultant and then as founder of her company (BI Brainz). The methods in the book have been tried and tested not only by Mico's team but also by thousands of people at some of the biggest companies in the world.

Although our recommended approach has been tested around the globe with lots of success, you may find that you can improve on or tweak it to better match your current environment or situation. Treat it as a starting point and solid foundation.

This book uses a methodology that Mico developed, called the *BI Dashboard Formula* (BIDF). To help you understand the process, we provide access to some of the templates and openly discuss our proven approach to developing these very powerful intelligent data visualizations. This method shows you the "what" (as in what data to display) as well as the "how" (as in how to add the right visuals to derive a powerful and compelling data viz).

Think of the data viz development process as being like building a house. First, you need to ensure you have the right location. Then you must develop a clear blueprint that shows exactly how the house will look. Last but not least, you lay the foundation and build the house. BIDF teaches you how to develop a visualization from start to finish.

We advise that you read this book from start to finish and avoid skipping any chapters, especially in Part II. Although the sky is the limit when it comes to building fancy data visualizations, creating useful data viz that provide true value by displaying intelligent data does require some background and a well-outlined process. A step-by-step process is explained in this book.

Ensuring Excellence in Your Data Visualization

Before you move on to the basics of building your data visualization, you should have some idea of what criteria make a data visualization excellent. An excellent data visualization has the following qualities:

- ✔ **It's visually appealing.** The advent of more sophisticated visual creation tools and the high quality of mobile apps have raised the bar very high on the user experience. It's only going to get higher with the evolution of technology such as Google Glass. Your visualization will go unused if it looks like it was designed with old technology.

- ✔ **It's scalable.** If your data viz is successful, others will want to use and leverage it. Be sure to build your visualization on a system that's scalable for accessibility and for future maintenance and modifications.

✔ **It gives the user the right information.** It's a problem when users focus on the visual or a particular feature and not on what they really need. Before creating a visualization, define exactly how it will be used, such as for self-service, drill-down, deep analysis, or executive overview.

✔ **It's accessible.** An accessible visualization is easy to use and can be modified easily when necessary. Also, the data must be accessible on any device, at any time, at any place. This feature is critical to user adoption.

✔ **It allows rapid development and deployment.** Gone are the days of waterfall (chart-type) projects and drawn-out data-viz deployments and builds. Users need their information today, and if you can't provide it in a timely fashion, they'll find other ways to get it.

Exploring Common Types of Data Visualizations

In This Chapter

▶ Understanding interactive graphics

▶ Selecting content for visualizations

▶ Looking at how different fields use visualizations

▶ Using cool infographics

*W*e've all seen impressive visualizations that make us feel humble. You may ask, "Could I do something like that?" Chances are that if you're creating a data visualization for the first time, the answer may be "not yet." Creating data visualizations, like anything else, requires you to acquire some basic information and build your knowledge over time.

This chapter presents different types of visualizations so that you can familiarize yourself with the many options you have for creating data visualizations of your own.

Understanding the Difference between Data Visualization and Infographics

To simplify the process of understanding visualizations, we focus on the two most popular types: data visualizations and infographics. Because the use of graphical data visualizations is growing quickly, there is a bit of disagreement about how to define a data visualization versus an infographic. You may believe that the definition is clear, but when you get into more complex visualizations, you can start to wonder.

In their book *Designing Data Visualizations* (O'Reilly Media), Noah Iliinsky and Julie Steele use the following three criteria to determine whether to call a graphic a data visualization or an infographic:

- **Method of generation:** This criterion refers to what goes into creating the graphic itself. If a lot of original illustrations are created to explain the data, for example, it's likely to be an infographic. You often see infographics with beautiful, elaborate images created to explain the information. Figure 2-1 shows an example created by Coleen Corcoran and Joe Prichard. You can see the original image at `http://thumbnails.visually.netdna-cdn.com/carland-a-century-of-motoring-in-america_50290aaca56d5.jpg`.

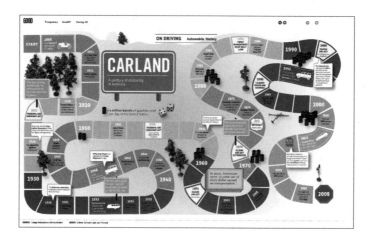

Figure 2-1: Carland displays history in an easy-to-follow way.

- **Quantity of data represented:** Typically, data visualizations have more and different kinds of data from infographics. Also, the data in data visualizations changes frequently to indicate changes in status. In addition, an infographic is less likely to include interactive numbers.

- **Degree of aesthetic treatment applied:** This criterion refers to the artfulness of the graphic. If a lot of design work has gone into displaying information, the graphic is likely to be an infographic.

We have another criterion to help you determine the difference between a data visualization and an infographic: whether the graphic is interactive or static.

An interactive graphic tells a different story each time new data is inserted. An interactive visualization helps you determine what the data is telling you. A static visualization depicts a data story that you want to explain to others. Figure 2-2 shows how coffee choices reflect one's personality. You can see the original image at `http://img7.joyreactor.com/pics/post/comics-thedoghousediaries-coffee-672107.png`.

Figure 2-2: A static visualization (infographic) isn't updated with new data.

You can use the information in Table 2-1 to determine whether you're working with an infographic or a data visualization. This table becomes useful when you want to decide what type of visualization to create for specific information and/or low-quality graphics.

Table 2-1	Data Visualizations versus Infographics	
	Data Visualization	*Infographic*
Method of generation	More numbers used	Original images created
Quantity of data	More data	Less data, more conclusions
Degree of aesthetic treatment	Less artful, more focused on information itself	More artful
Interactive versus static	Interactive (data changes)	Static (data remains fixed)

Read on to find out what types of content you can put in an infographic or data visualization.

Picking the Right Content Type

When you're creating a data visualization to tell the story of your data, you can use many content types other than text and numbers. The key is to select visuals that are not only attractive but that also match the data you have. This is not an insignificant task. Your data viz will benefit from careful consideration of a variety of different content types.

Following are several to consider:

- **Graph:** An x and y axis is used to depict data as a visualization.
- **Diagram:** A visual that shows how something works.
- **Timeline:** A chronology is depicted on a graph to show how something happens or changes.
- **Template:** A guide for something that a user needs to fill in or develop.
- **Checklist:** A list of tasks to be completed that can be crossed off when they have been accomplished.

- ✔ **Flow chart:** A sequential set of instructions that show how something works.

- ✔ **Metaphor:** Comparisons of two dissimilar things for the purpose of making a vivid description.

- ✔ **Mind map:** Maps that enable you to show the big picture and the details of a topic on one sheet of paper. The main topic is in the center and the subtopics radiate out from it. Figure 2-3 shows an example of a mind map about the best-selling book *Brain Rules* by John Medina (Pear Press). It was created using the MindMeister software (`https://www.mindmeister.com/100879355/brain-rules-12-principles-for-surviving-and-thriving-at-work-home-and-school`).

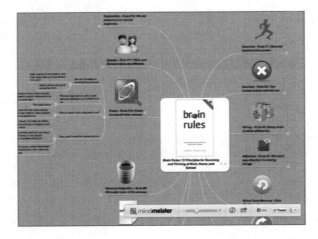

Figure 2-3: A mind map is one content type you might use for a data viz.

When you see a visualization that contains interesting content types, you should clip the image and save it to a file for future reference. That way, you'll always have images that really inspire you. You can also refer to Chapter 15, which provides a list of hand-picked resources to keep you informed and inspired.

One caveat: Make sure that your data fits the visualization that you choose. Don't try to shoehorn data in just for the sake of art.

Appreciating Interactive Data Visualizations

Sophisticated software allows people to do analysis today that they only dared dream about five years ago. Couple this with mounting data stores, and you have an interesting choice. You can put your head in the sand and hope that the data stops multiplying, or you can work at making it a valuable asset.

Some companies choose to ignore the growing stacks of data and continue to rely on standard methods like spreadsheets that offer little customer insight. Others take a leap and bring in software that helps them analyze both their structured and their unstructured data (such as social media data). They can then create data visualizations that help them make more educated, fact-based business decisions and predictions.

The jury is still out as to whether most corporations will take full advantage of their data for competitive purposes. Companies that do realize that being able to analyze many forms of data at the same time in the form of interactive visualizations have a competitive advantage. From understanding the sentiments of their customers to examining their buying habits, the possibilities to get ahead of one's competitors by viewing one's data are endless!

Companies that take advantage of their available data by putting it into interactive data visualizations can reap the following benefits:

- **Self-service:** Users can manipulate the data to find out specific things they need to know.

- **Immediacy:** Users can be alerted to situations that require immediate attention.

- **Improved collaboration:** When everyone on a team is looking at the same data, the team can solve problems more easily.

- **Simplicity:** Users are presented with only the key elements that enable them to get both the big picture and the details in one visualization.

- **Insight:** Users can glean important revelations about the company's performance from a good interactive visualization.

- **Depiction of patterns:** Patterns make it easier for users to analyze the data and identify trends. It is unlikely that users would be able to recognize patterns when presented with millions of lines of data in a spreadsheet; visualizations make it easier to identify patterns at a glance.

Groups that use data visualization receive many of these benefits. Next, we look at how different fields use data visualizations to their advantage.

Observing Visualizations in Different Fields

Many fields of study now use data visualization to provide insight to their audiences about all types of data — political, financial, scientific, and historical. Like anything that gains popularity, you can find both good and bad examples of data visualizations (see Chapter 13).

Politics and government

In the field of politics and government, data analysis has taken center stage. Government agencies are combining social media data with demographic information to inform decisions and convey information. Figure 2-4 shows a couple of visualizations that describe how recovery funds are distributed. You can see the original image at `www.recovery.gov/Pages/default.aspx`.

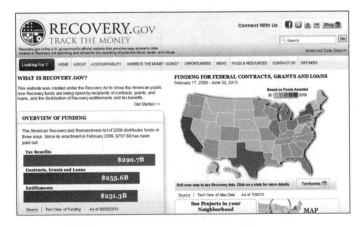

Figure 2-4: Government Recovery data by zip code.

Finance/social economics

Many financial institutions use visualizations to inform their clients about their own portfolios as well as current economic issues, such as interest rates and tax implications. Social data is also a common topic for visualizations — things like Tweets, shares, and check-ins, as shown in Figure 2-5. The original image is at `http://blog.backupify.com/2012/04/05/what-is-social-data-worth/`.

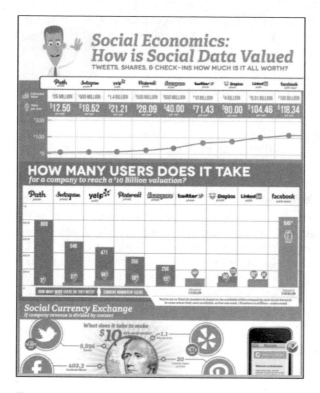

Figure 2-5: The value of social data according to Backupify.com.

Science

Science has always relied on some kind of visual to depict information. Advances in technology allow much more data to be analyzed at one time so that patterns can be more easily identified. Figure 2-6 shows a visualization that plots the occurrence of hurricanes since 1851. You can clearly see that some areas are more heavily affected than others. You can see the original image at www.theguardian.com/news/datablog/2012/oct/29/every-hurricane-visualised-since-1851.

History

Historical data is a great use of visualizations because it incorporates a large amount of data in a relatively small space. For example, you can follow the evolution of an idea or the growth of a company. You can also choose the segments to fit the data instead of forcing the data into some artificial designation.

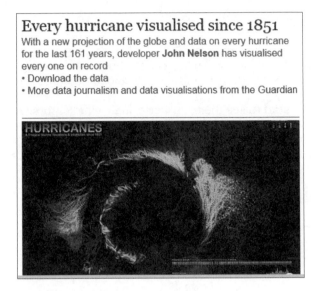

Figure 2-6: The visualization of hurricane data shows that hurricanes occur more frequently in some places than in others.

For example, Figure 2-7 is an infographic showing how modes of communication have changed over the years. Notice that the segments of time are not uniform. However, if you are showing the growth of something, like the car industry, you could designate uniform periods to show which periods had the most explosive growth over the century. Check out the original image at http://visual.ly/communication-through-ages.

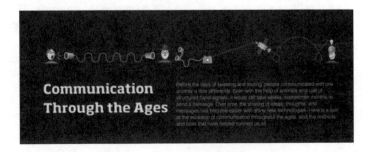

Figure 2-7: Historical look at communication.

Using Dashboards

As we discuss in several chapters of the book, Mico's company BIBrainz.com uses her Business Intelligence Dashboard Formula (BIDF) to help users around the world build their dashboards and understand their data.

Dashboards allow staff to see their Key Performance Indicators (KPIs) and important alerts on one screen. They have become increasingly popular because of the growing amount of data companies need to harness. Dashboards enable companies to put measures from different departments in one graphic.

Following are some benefits of dashboards:

- They remove the need to update manual calculations.
- They focus on the measures that are most important to the audience.
- They alert stakeholders to action(s) that must be taken.
- They increase productivity by showing the most important data on one screen so that users don't have to go searching for it.

How do you know whether you're on the right track when creating your first dashboard? Here are three questions to ask yourself:

- **Will any stakeholders champion the use of the dashboard going forward?** Unless some people believe in the data and want the dashboard to be used, the dashboard could languish unnoticed after the first flurry of interest.

- **Will someone update and maintain the numbers in the dashboard?** You need to make sure that whoever looks at the data is seeing current data that takes changes in company direction into account. Having a dashboard that reflects bad or outdated data is as unhelpful as having no data.

- **Is the dashboard truly easy to understand?** This issue probably is the most important one that we cover in this book. If the visualization in the dashboard is confusing, no one will use it, no matter how pretty it is.

Discovering Infographics

Infographics have gained great favor of late. If done well, they can illuminate a problem and tell an interesting story. Infographics have generated great interest on the Internet because of their ability to entertain as well as enlighten.

Infographics use design rules to artfully display text, numbers, metaphors, and other data types. You should use a few key guidelines when you're planning your own infographic or evaluating one:

- **Make the infographic easy to understand.** First and foremost, an infographic should be simple. If the information isn't clear or leads to confusion, you've failed.

- **Make it accurate.** Infographics reflect actual data. The artwork must accurately reflect the data and carefully report the trends or patterns of the data. Double-check your work.

- **Provide your sources.** Data sources typically are listed at the bottom of an infographic. If you want yours to have credibility, list all the places where the data was gathered.

- **Choose complementary colors.** An infographic should be eye-catching. If you have trouble determining what colors to use, many online tools can help. For more information using color in your visualizations, read Chapter 10.

- **Make it worthwhile.** Although it's true that infographics can be frivolous or silly, most business users are looking for solid information. Take the time to create something that others will want to share.

Examining different types of infographics

Several types of infographics are currently popular. The following list can help you choose the right type for the information you're trying to illustrate:

- **Case study:** If you've conducted a specific inquiry about a particular topic and want to share the results, try a case study. In the context of an infographic, a case study shows the goals, objectives, and outcome of a particular campaign or action plan.

- **Chronology:** The content of a chronology follows a logical, dated order, as shown in Figure 2-8. Use this type of infographic if you want to recount something like the history of a product or the growth of an industry. You can view the chronology shown in the figure at `http://educationcloset.com/wp-content/uploads/2012/05/creativity-infographic.jpg`.

- **Comparison:** When you're trying to show the difference between one item and another, try a comparison. Figure 2-9 shows a comparison of iOS 6 and iOS 7 icons; in the comparison you can see that some changes make sense, whereas others seem to change simply for the sake of change. See the original image at `http://mashable.com/2013/06/12/ios-7-apps-comparison`.

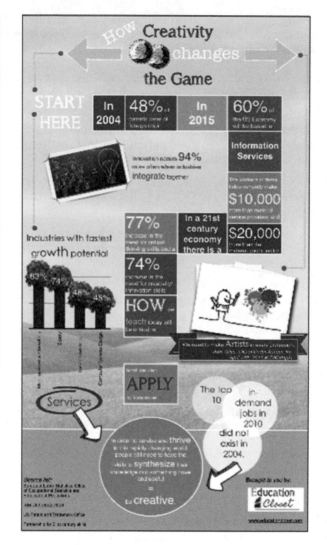

Figure 2-8: This chronology illustrates the effect of creativity in industry.

✔ **Compilation:** If you want to inform your audience about a key topic and make it memorable, use a compilation of information as an infographic. A compilation refers to a collection of information that is gathered from a variety of sources into one cohesive whole.

✔ **Expert advice:** Dispensing expert advice in an infographic is a great way to establish yourself as an expert. It also "helps the medicine go down" if you're recommending something difficult.

Figure 2-9: A comparison of icons used in iOS 6 and iOS 7.

✔ **How-to information:** Presenting information in a sequential manner is a great way to educate your audience. Infographics often use visuals to get the message across, as shown in Figure 2-10. The original image is available at www.stack.com/2012/06/20/how-to-properly-use-sunscreen.

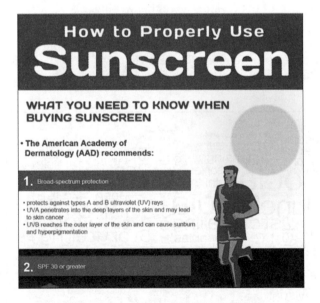

Figure 2-10: The how-to infographic describes the proper use of sunscreen.

Sometimes, infographics are just for fun. Don't hesitate to use humor when you display data on a lighthearted subject. It's okay to entertain your users as you provide information. Just be sure to represent the data accurately.

Taking advantage of online infographic tools

If you want to try your hand at infographics, a lot of great online tools are available. Many of them supply graphic and design templates that simplify things for do-it-yourselfers.

Here are some tools that you may want to consider:

- **Piktochart** (http://piktochart.com): Create your own infographics by using templates. Free and fee versions are available.

- **Venngage** (https://venngage.com): This tool is a great way to create infographics. It doesn't work with Internet Explorer but does work with Mozilla Firefox and Google Chrome. Free and fee versions are available.

- **Creatly** (http://creately.com): This tool is useful for creating good-looking diagrams. Free and fee versions are available.

- **easel.ly** (http://easel.ly): This tool, which has easy drag-and-drop features, is in beta testing as of this writing.

- **Wordle** (www.wordle.net/create): This tool lets you create a free word cloud for any URL. The size of the word displayed indicates what topics are covered most. Figure 2-11 shows a Wordle cloud created for Stephanie's blog, Marketing Message Mindset.com.

Figure 2-11: A Wordle cloud created for Stephanie's blog.

What about you?

Just for fun, you may want to check out a tool called What About Me? that creates a personalized infographic. You can find it at www. intel.com/content/www/us/en/ what-about-me/what-about-me. html. The figure shows the landing page.

The tool visualizes your digital life by using your Facebook, Twitter, and YouTube accounts. The visuals are well done and created almost instantly. The result will probably tell you things about your digital life that even you didn't know.

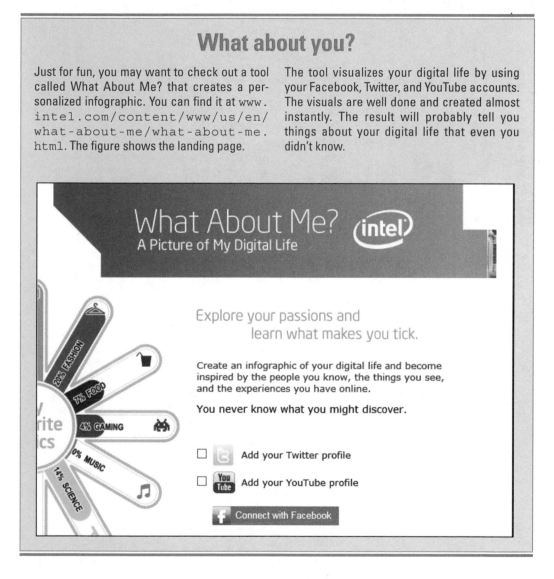

3

Knowing What You Must about Big Data

In This Chapter

▶ Understanding Big Data

▶ Seeing how Big Data is used in business

▶ Choosing tools for visualization

*A*nyone who spends time online instinctively knows that data is continuing to grow at a rapid rate. But the magnitude of data growth may shock you. According to Marcia Conner, in her article "Data on Big Data," 90 percent of all the data in the world has been created in the last two years. (See the article at `http://marciaconner.com/blog/data-on-big-data`.)

If you're doing business today, it's no secret that you're bombarded by all kinds of data. The key is to use this data as an opportunity to create a competitive advantage. In other words, if you take steps to harness and analyze the data you have, you will be ahead of many of your competitors who are still waiting to figure out what to do with their Big Data.

Volume

SCALE OF DATA

Defining Big Data

Suddenly, everyone is talking about the presence of Big Data and its impact. Hasn't there always been a steady stream of data that companies can employ? What makes the data so "big" that its mere presence can't be managed?

These questions and many others probably come to mind. The best way to answer them is to think about how you currently interact with devices throughout your day:

- ✔ Communicate via smartphones
- ✔ Send reports, proposals, and contracts digitally
- ✔ Buy products via online accounts
- ✔ Use credit cards at retail stores
- ✔ Monitor your car and house with various electronic devices such as temperature gauges and dashboard computers

Don't forget that data is generated when you interact on social media and in search engines. Most of this data was unavailable a mere 20 years ago.

Every one of the preceding activities throws off mountains of data. The retailer sees what you buy; the smartphone provider knows who you call; the car dashboard records your driving habits. You (and your customers) are a walking mass of data. All this acquired information is what we're talking about when we say *Big Data*.

Seeing How Big Data Changes Business

It's interesting to note that Big Data changes the way employees work. Here are a few examples:

- ✔ Salespeople can access data and make decisions about offers right from the customer's location.
- ✔ Customer service representatives can access information about buying habits and needs while they're online or on the phone with customers.
- ✔ Financial managers can access specific data to meet their needs, and marketing departments can drill down to specific campaign details.

We're sure that you can see the value Big Data brings to any organization that makes an effort to use it. You get not only productivity gains but also faster insight into your problems. Interestingly, most CEOs used to believe that their fortunes were strictly in their customer lists. Now, many are coming to believe that the inclusion of Big Data and the attendant insights it brings will be the source of their fortunes.

With Big Data, you can become customer-centric in ways you never could before. You can go beyond transactional reports about customer buying habits and drill down to customer sentiment and motivation. This chapter looks at what Big Data is and how you can harness it to create data visualizations. The opportunities are limitless.

One thing that businesses should focus on is the fact that they can now get answers to questions they couldn't previously ask, which makes asking the right questions a very important factor in Big Data analysis. You're only as good as the questions you ask.

Getting to know your customers

Companies today have the opportunity to "know" each customer's individual habits. Instead of creating artificial groups of customers who may have some similar interests, businesses can effectively segment and customize their offers to each customer. By knowing customers' habits, companies can not only target niches more accurately but also uncover new markets for their goods, understand customer needs more fully, and extend well-timed special offers.

Here are three major benefits of using Big Data to understand your customers:

- **Customer satisfaction:** You can create fans who are loyal and who speak about your products to others on social media. This situation creates a sales force that money can't buy.

- **More money per customer:** Offering just the right product at the right time increases buying.

- **Retention:** You keep customers longer by showing them that you understand their needs and can provide them with products that meet those needs.

Companies that use Big Data can extract value in several new ways. The following key factors shed light on why companies believe that Big Data presents such a great opportunity:

- **New tools are available.** You can use the tools that are now available to analyze this new data in near real time. These tools include data sensors that collect massive amounts of information about how machines and electronics are performing.

- **New insights are possible.** Being able to analyze the data provides the capability to extract major insights that can increase profits.

- **New types of data are being generated.** Some of social data deals with customer sentiment, which is invaluable to companies. Customer sentiment data lets companies know what offers will succeed because they learn how customers talk about and review their products.

- **New developments make cloud storage a reality.** Warehousing data is less an issue now that businesses can use cloud storage, which is cheaper and just as accessible.

All this sounds pretty good. But Big Data also presents a few challenges. The next section looks at the essence of the problem.

Discovering the Four V's

To understand the challenges of Big Data, the Business Intelligence (BI) community commonly designates what it calls the *Four V's:*

- ✔ **Volume:** Tons of data is generated around the globe, and the volume will continue to increase exponentially in the coming years.

- ✔ **Variety:** Different and new kinds of structured and unstructured data (such as social media data) are being created. (For more information, see "Collecting structured and unstructured data," later in this chapter.)

- ✔ **Velocity:** The pace at which data is mounting is accelerating, and companies' ability to analyze it in real time is crucial to the development of tangible offers that turn shoppers into actual customers.

- ✔ **Veracity:** *Veracity* refers to the trustworthiness of data. Is the data that's being generated valid? When analyzing data about customer sentiment on social media, for example, can you trust everything that's been written?

IBM has created an excellent infographic illustrating the Four V's, as shown in Figure 3-1. (You can find the image at `http://cdn.dashburst.com/wp-content/uploads/2013/07/the-four-v-s-of-big-data.jpg`.)

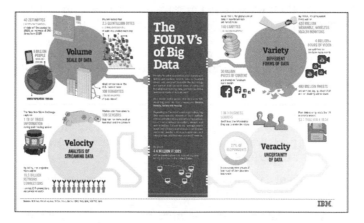

Figure 3-1: The Four V's.

These four factors influence the management of Big Data. Whether you're a small-business owner or an executive of a major corporation, you are affected by the onslaught of data. The following sections dig a bit deeper into the kinds of data you will be working with.

Collecting structured and unstructured data

Data collected in the past was structured and could fit into neat rows and columns. An example of this would be an Excel spreadsheet with delimited data (data that was separated by a specific character, such as a comma). Most internal information specialists were content to display this data (such as customer records) in long spreadsheets. They were tasked with reporting what the data said, and everyone used the same results. There was no opportunity to visualize the story that the data told to extract valuable insights. The data wasn't interactive and didn't allow for customization. It was valuable to a point, but there was no way to understand what the customer thought about the product after they bought it. You would only know *that* the product had been bought. And that data is only one part of the puzzle.

Today, companies are facing a mountain of a new type of data: unstructured data, which doesn't always come in a neat package. Following are a few examples of this type of data:

✔ **Opinions:** Opinions are gathered by review sites such as Yelp, shown in Figure 3-2. You can access the reviews directly or use a tool that scrapes the data from the site so that you can put that data in your own data-viz tool.

Figure 3-2: Restaurant reviews on Yelp.

✔ **Visuals:** Visuals are chosen by users of sites such as Pinterest, shown in Figure 3-3. In the case of Pinterest, you can access the site to see what images about and by your company have been pinned by customers who are searching for your company's name. You may have data about which of your company's pins are being re-pinned by others as well as data about people who have seen your company's product or image elsewhere on the web and have pinned it directly to Pinterest for others to find.

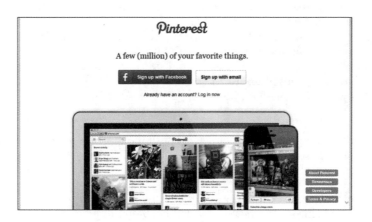

Figure 3-3: The Pinterest site can generate a lot of data for a company.

✔ **Smartphone data:** Phone records, e-mails, and other search data are available from your phone.

This unstructured content represents data that's incredibly valuable to any online business. The key to using the data is to utilize software programs (such SAP) that enable you to combine structured data with unstructured data to gain a greater understanding of the business and its customers. From this analysis, companies can begin to make predictions about customer behavior and revenue generation.

Typically, organizations that use unstructured data use natural language processing software to analyze it.

Ensuring the use of quality data

The quality of your data, not your choice of tool, determines the value of your visualization. In a 2013 article in the *Harvard Business Review* titled "When Data Visualization Works — and When It Doesn't," author Jim Stikeleather pointed out three elements that affect the efficacy of data:

✔ **Data quality:** Obviously, if your data is incomplete or full of errors, your data visualization will be useless. But it's not always easy to determine what data is missing and, therefore, how reliable the predictions you make with it will be. It's important to pay attention to the quality of your data up front to make sure that your conclusions are usable. Work with your IT department and major stakeholders to determine as much about your data as you can. Find out about its origins and how often it is updated.

- **Context:** Context refers to your ability to draw conclusions from your data. If you don't understand how the data was sourced, how current it is, and so on, you risk drawing faulty conclusions from it.

- **Biases:** It's important to acknowledge any biases you have about the data before you create your visualization. Do you want the conclusions to support a pet theory? Are you making the data visualization look a certain way to support your conclusions? You must divest yourself of these notions before you begin.

Regarding biases, when you look at any data visualization, it's a good idea to ask yourself whether the data was created by someone who may have a stake in a certain outcome. Sometimes, the developer's bias may be unconscious. Make an agreement with the major stakeholders that the data you use must be certified by IT so that you avoid any bias that might be introduced when the stakeholders themselves provide the data.

Avoiding Dying by Tool Choice

Throughout this book, we state that the most important thing to focus on is data preparation, not tools. That said, we understand that it's easy to be distracted by the variety of tools that are available for creating visualization.

All tools are not created equal. Tying yourself to a tool before you know what needs to be displayed is a recipe for failure. If your company has already chosen a specific tool, obviously, you have to figure out how to work with that one. But if you have the freedom to decide on a tool, make sure to let the data drive your choice.

When choosing a tool, it's important to know what separates truly advanced tools from simpler ones. In a 2012 Forrester Wave report titled "Advanced Data Visualization (ADV) Platforms," Bob Evelson and Noel Yuhanna outlined several points that separate the current crop of advanced tools from older, less powerful tools:

- **Dynamic data content:** The data is interactive and can be updated regularly to show changes.

- **Visual querying:** Users can click icons and other visuals to update the data.

- **Multiple-dimension, linked visualization:** Multiple types of data can be linked to show different dimensions.

✔ **Animated visualization:** An animated visualization enables you to quickly go to the data you want to see so that you don't have to spend time clicking through data that's not relevant to you.

✔ **Personalization:** The software assigns different levels of access to the data as well as access to different slices of that data based on the particular user.

✔ **Business-actionable alerts:** The software triggers alerts that can notify various stakeholders when appropriate.

You may want to evaluate your tools based on these measures. You can access the full report by downloading the PDF at www.sas.com/news/analysts/Forrester_Wave_Advanced_Data_Visualization_Platforms_Q3_2012.pdf.

We can't know which tool is right for you, of course. Tableau and QlikView have growing adoption rates, so we discuss them in more detail in the following sections.

Tableau

Tableau has gained popularity because it's an easy-to-use, drag-and-drop software tool. Both free and fee-based versions of the software are available.

The free version (www.tableausoftware.com/public), shown in Figure 3-4, allows users to craft public data to tell a story. Typically, it's used by individuals or small companies. It's optimized for the iPad and Android devices.

Figure 3-4: Tableau for Enterprise.

The fee-based version (www.tableausoftware.com) is for larger organizations that want to plug in their own confidential data. A free trial period is available for this version.

QlikView

QlikView (http://qlikview.com; see Figure 3-5) is relatively new software that has gained favor quickly. It also has free and fee-based versions. It is known for its ease of use and wide range of tools. It can be used by both small and large organizations.

Figure 3-5: The QlikView homepage.

Part II

Mastering Basic Data Visualization Concepts

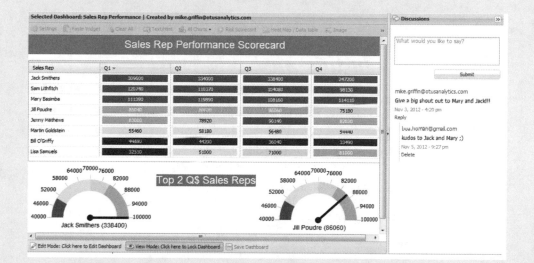

Want to have a handy list of unbreakable rules for placing text in your data visualizations? Visit www.dummies.com/extras/datavisualization to see our "Ten Unbreakable Rules for Using Text in a Data Visualization."

In this part...

- ✓ Find out how to choose and use charts effectively from a variety of choices, such as diagrams, pie charts, graphs, and timelines.

- ✓ Learn to add the proper context to your chart so that the viewer doesn't have to guess what your data viz means.

- ✓ Understand how details such as font sizes, text labeling, and patterns can help your users understand what you're presenting in your visualization.

Using Charts Effectively

In This Chapter

▶ Keeping charts simple

▶ Using charts that are clear to users

▶ Knowing when to use dials

*M*ost people are introduced to charts pretty early in their school careers. Teachers use charts for attendance, seating, spelling, history lessons, and so on. This is probably why, unless you're a math major, you hope you never have to deal with charts again.

But it's time to take a second look. New tools have made it much easier to turn raw data into a good-looking chart. In addition, as a person facing the Big Data age, you probably can't escape it anyway. It's time to embrace data visualizations.

This chapter looks at different types of charts and their use. You need to know which charts are best for beginners and which ones to avoid.

Deciding Which Charts to Use and When to Use Them

The purpose of a chart is to package information in a way that makes it quickly understandable. The thing that makes charts so useful is that they provide a quickly recognizable shape for your data. Think about that for a moment. Each graph you create has its own shape that is dictated by the data inside it. It's a visual explanation of a story.

A good chart can be understood at a glance. The information is communicated by telling you, for example, whether something is going up or going down — for example, whether prices are rising or falling. If you want to know whether a widget is selling, you can consult a chart that shows the trend line.

Understanding where newbies should start

When you're new to a subject, you seek guidelines that help you master the content. Creating charts is no exception. Here are a few rules to get you off to a fast start:

- **Employ simplicity.** Simplicity is the key to creating effective data visualizations. You should focus on using simple charts that are easy to digest. You won't get points for most amount of data displayed.

- **Display only the most important information.** When you're new to charting, you may want to put in a lot of information so that you don't leave out anything of value. Resist this urge, because people can take in only so much information before their eyes glaze over.

- **Require little explanation.** Don't make things so complicated that your users require a manual to understand what you're trying to convey. If you can't get something at a glance, it's too complicated for your reader.

- **Don't overload your data.** It's important to avoid overloading your data visualization, but the trend toward the use of mobile devices makes this practice even more important. Mobile devices reduce the screen real estate to almost half of what's available on a desktop. Typically, a visualization isn't manipulated on a mobile phone; it's only viewed.

- **Stay away from 3-D.** At some point in your data career, you may become a whiz at depicting charts in 3-D. We recommend that you avoid this type of chart, however, until you get more experience under your belt.

Next, you want to know what elements make up a good chart so that you can incorporate those elements:

- **Labels:** Labels are so important, yet many people forget to add them. Whether it's the title of the chart, the chart legend, or the labels for the axes, letting users know what is being displayed is vital. Users typically look at the title of a chart before the actual chart, so be aware that you need one.

- **Color:** Choosing the correct colors for your chart is critical. Whether you are displaying different quantities or pointing out specific measures, choosing appropriate colors is an absolute must. At a glance, most users are likely to focus on brighter colors first, sometimes completely overlooking less highlighted colors, such as gray. Strategically using the right colors in your chart guides your users and adds value by enabling them to decide what to focus on first.

✔ **Chart Type:** Choosing the correct chart to tell the story of your data is quite a challenge. It's not surprising that the use of pie charts is so highly debated. Many newbies tend to go with what makes their data look pretty, often choosing the wrong chart for the wrong reasons. There are, in fact, very specific uses for the different chart styles, many of which are covered in this chapter.

Figure 4-1 shows how you might set up a chart to display some data on the x- and y-axes. In the figure, each axis is clearly labeled in its correct position.

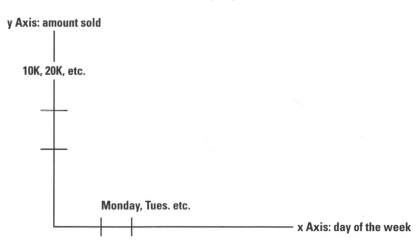

Figure 4-1: A simple chart with an appropriate title and axis labels.

✔ **Labels:** Users have to know what they're seeing at a glance. Make sure to include labels for everything that isn't readily apparent.

Always include the source of the data at the bottom of the chart if the chart will be viewed outside your company. Read more about copyrights in Chapter 11.

Choosing simple and effective charts

Although you have many chart types to choose among, we recommend starting with some of the simple and most commonly used charts for the most chance for success: bar and column charts, line charts, and pie charts. No doubt you're familiar with them and have seen many examples. In the following sections, we discuss these chart types and show you when to use them.

Bar and column charts

Some people use the term *bar chart* when speaking about a chart that shows the data horizontally or vertically; others call a chart that displays the data vertically a *column chart.* Whatever you call them, these charts are best used for comparisons.

Figure 4-2 shows an example of a column chart. (You can also see the image at `http://www.smartdraw.com/examples/view/future+wealth+holder%27s+gender+shift+bar+chart.`) Notice that the chart is simple, with a title, a labeled axis, and clear labels to show what the columns represent.

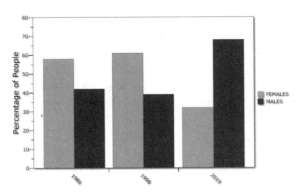

Figure 4-2: Column chart.

 When you use a column chart, be sure to shorten or use smaller labels on your x-axis below each bar to ensure they display horizontally. Utilizing longer labels will result in needing to display the title vertically (as shown in Figure 4-2), which is hard for the user to read.

Line charts

A *line chart* connects data points over a period of time, as shown in Figure 4-3. (You can also find the image at `http://www.smartdraw.com/examples/view/cost+of+crude+oil+line+chart.`)

Line charts are best used for something like a trend to show movement. These charts are easy to read and fairly easy to create. This type of chart should be one of your staples.

Pie charts

The use of pie charts is controversial, and the debate is more than a decade old. Just type the words **avoid pie chart** in a search engine, and you'll literally find more than 1 million entries. One of the best-known data

design experts, Edward Tufte, refers to pie charts as "dumb" in his book
The Visual Display of Quantitative Information (Graphics Press). Tufte argues
that pie charts are dumb because they fail to show comparisons and trends
as well as bar or line charts do. Many experts argue that the eyes are not
good at estimating areas, which you must do when viewing a pie chart.

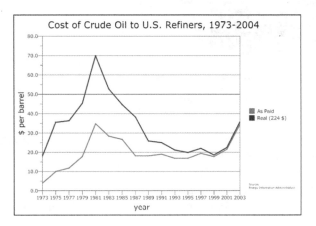

Figure 4-3: Line chart.

Although we agree with the main argument that the human eye isn't very
good at estimating areas, it's hard to ignore the fact that pie charts remain
among the most beloved types of charts. We believe that it's primarily
because of their round shape.

The more you tell data visualization authors to avoid pie charts, the more
they want to use them, either because their users request them or because
they hope to add some variety to their visualizations.

We believe that you can indeed use pie charts as effective data visualizations
if — and only if — you stick to the purpose they were meant to serve and
follow the guidelines we provide in this section.

By definition, pie charts are circular charts divided into slices, with the size
of each slice showing the relative value. In other words, at a glance, it should
be easy to see which slices of the pie contribute the most and least to the
whole pie. Well, it's not quite as easy as you may think.

Take a look at the two most common ways pie charts are misused:

> ✔ **Too many slices are displayed.** We recommend that you limit the number
> of pie slices to five. Displaying additional slices that are too small to be
> sorted will only distract the user from the main point. Figure 4-4 shows a
> pie chart displaying how much (by percentage) each revenue stream has
> contributed to the company's overall revenue in the last quarter.

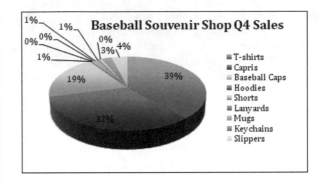

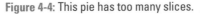

Figure 4-4: This pie has too many slices.

At a glance, it's clear that T-shirts, capris, and baseball caps combined account for 90 percent of the company's sales. What isn't so clear are the products that make up the remaining 10 percent of the revenue.

Figure 4-5 shows a better way to display the same data. Notice that the other products are combined in a slice titled Other. This makes the chart easier to digest. You highlight the top contributors and show the contributions of the additional slices as a single sector.

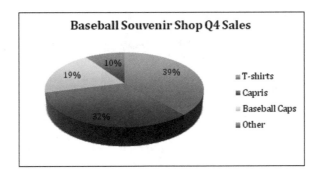

Figure 4-5: The insignificant contributors have been combined into the Other group.

✏ **Slices of equal value are displayed.** This is another common mistake. The pie chart in Figure 4-5 has fewer than five slices, but because the value of some of the slices are relatively the same, it's hard to compare the actual contribution of those individual slices relative to another one another.

Figure 4-6 displays the same data from Figure 4-5 in a column chart that has been set to sort in ascending order.

Notice how much easier it is to see which products have contributed the most revenue, even if the differences in some of the values are very slim?

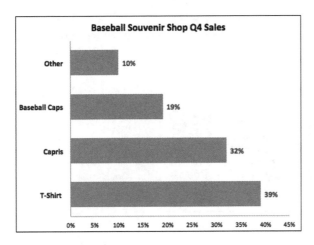

Baseball Souvenir Shop Q4 Sales

Figure 4-6: The data is sorted in ascending order.

Unless you're developing static data visualizations such as infographics or a yearly report in which the data isn't updated dynamically, avoid using pie charts. The reality is that most Big Data visualizations are going to be updated dynamically from some real-time database, making it nearly impossible to control the data output. The risk of breaking one, if not both, of the rules of pie charts we provide in this section is very high; ultimately, the risk isn't worth making the data hard to read.

Using gauges and scorecards to monitor

Here's a question you probably thought you wouldn't see in this chapter on using charts: Do you always need to create a chart for your data? The answer is "Not always." You can use other devices instead, such as a gauge or scorecard. People are familiar with gauges because we use them in everyday life. You glance at your car's gas gauge to determine how much gas you have, for example.

In data visualizations, gauges are often used to monitor the status of key performance indicators or something with known data parameters. If you know the lowest and highest measurements, you can use tick marks to

Who created these charts?

You may not have thought about it before, but somebody had to invent the first bar, line, and pie charts. That person was William Playfair, a Scottish engineer who used the first pie chart in 1801. If you want to impress your friends with trivia, this item is useful to know.

display them and use a pointer to show where the data is at the present time. Figure 4-7 shows examples of how gauges are used to display data. (See the image at www.infragistics.com/help/topic/780FF79B-3E5A-40B3-9AA3-3EB8A2683798.)

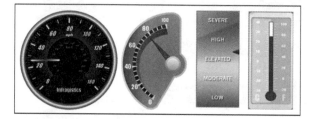

Figure 4-7: Gauges.

Just like pie charts, gauges have their critics. Some people believe that a gauge doesn't provide historical data, so it's not as useful as it could be. The same is true for scorecards.

Considered to be a separate form of data visualization altogether (depending on the source), scorecards are also used to monitor measurements. As opposed to a gauge, which is limited to monitoring a single measurement, a single scorecard can monitor multiple measurements at the same time, which makes it more useful to more users. Figure 4-8 show how a scorecard can be used to view sales data across two quarters (see the image at www.otusanalytics.com/wp/wp-content/uploads/2013/01/salesRepPerformanceScorecard.png).

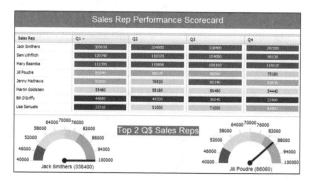

Figure 4-8: Scorecard.

Finding online tools for chart making

When you're creating your first chart, you'll probably use Microsoft Excel. But you can use many online tools to accomplish the same task. Here are a few that you may want to consider:

- ✏ **Rich Chart Live** (`www.richchartlive.com/RichChartLive`): Available in both free and fee-based versions

- ✏ **ChartGo** (`www.chartgo.com/index.jsp`): Free

- ✏ **ChartGizmo** (`http://chartgizmo.com`): Free

- ✏ **Online Chart Tool** (`www.onlinecharttool.com`): Free

Dipping Into Less-Common Charts

We've provided a clear list of charts to stick with if you're new to charting. We use the KISS acronym, which means "Keep It Simple, Superstar!" We realize, however, that you'll get bored using the same vanilla charts, as we all do, and you'll want to make your data visualization "sexy" by venturing into more exotic chart territory.

While you're trying to find sexier charts to display your data, it's important to keep in mind that the ultimate goal of any data visualization is to take a huge data set and display intelligence data in the form of charts, text, and other visual elements that are easy for the user to digest.

Here are three common chart types that lure newbies with their sex appeal but provide little to no value to readers, who are often confused by them:

- ✏ **Radar charts:** Also known as spider or star charts because of their appearance, radar charts are designed to plot the values of different categories along a separate axis that starts from the center and ends in the outer ring, as shown in Figure 4-9.

  Although this cobweb of a chart definitely adds some sex appeal to your Big Data visualization, most users have no idea how to read the data. They get confused trying to decipher it without some accompanying text. We advise sticking to a bar or column chart instead.

- ✏ **Candlestick charts:** Candlestick charts were invented for the stock market and are used to describe the price movements of derivatives, securities, or currency over time. Stock-market data is the only type of data for which this chart type should be used. Understanding when a candlestick is high or low isn't a concept that most readers are familiar with, so this type of chart will only serve to confuse them.

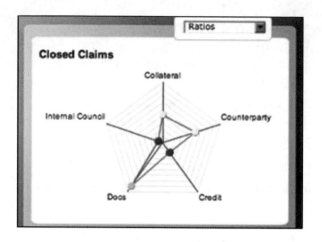

Figure 4-9: Radar chart.

Figure 4-10 shows a candlestick chart displaying stock-related data. (You can find the image at www.visifire.com/documentation/ Visifire_Documentation/Charts/Common_Tasks/creating_ candlestick_chart_using_axisxlabel.htm.)

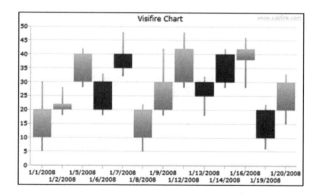

Figure 4-10: Candlestick chart.

 **Waterfall charts:** These charts display the effect of positive and negative changes on a specific value over time. Waterfall charts are nicknamed "flying bricks" because they appear to be flying in midair.

Figure 4-11 shows a typical waterfall chart displaying financial profit/loss data. Colors on the bars indicate a negative or positive change in value, so you can easily see the $100,000 plunge that the company's profit took (from $420,000 to $320,000) and all the contribution costs in between.

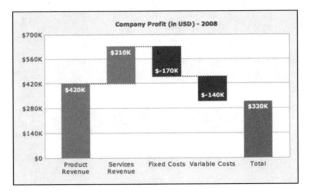

Figure 4-11: A waterfall chart.

We recommend that you avoid using radar and candlestick charts. On the other hand, we advise using waterfall charts after you've mastered the simple charts we recommend earlier in this chapter. Waterfall charts aren't all bad, and their meaning isn't difficult for users to discern. When you do decide to use these charts, we highly recommend putting some text at the bottom to help readers who are encountering this type of chart for the first time.

Don't get carried away trying to fit your data into a sexy chart. Instead, focus on the message you're trying to convey. Charts were made for data; data wasn't made for charts. The message of your data should always dictate the charts you use. If you choose a sexy chart and then try to fit in data, you almost always confuse users, which lowers user adoption.

5

Adding a Little Context

In This Chapter

▶ Understanding the role of text in data visualizations

▶ Getting the most out of text

▶ Analyzing text

*R*emember the saying "A picture is worth a thousand words"? Well, although this saying may hold true for museum art, it doesn't apply to most data visualizations. One of the main reasons why users request data visualizations is to get away from tons of reports with loads of data and text that either take too long to interpret or are too difficult to understand.

If you want to create truly powerful data visualizations, adding some context in the form of text is one of the most effective ways to communicate your data. Take a stop sign, for example. Have you ever noticed that besides the unique shape and color of it, the text STOP is right in the middle? (See Figure 5-1.) Globally this is probably one of the most recognized signs — identifiable just by its shape and color. The text on the sign text just makes it that much easier to recognize what the sign is telling you. There is no room for misinterpretation; the stop sign is a good example of using text to add smart context to a visualization.

You should apply the same practice to your data visualizations. You shouldn't make the assumption that a visualization that's clear to one user will be as clear to 100 other users. This is where adding some context to your data visualization becomes important. Adding context in the form of text is a foolproof way to ensure that all your users get the same message.

Figure 5-1: Users recognize what a stop sign is communicating based on the shape, the color, and the text.

Adding any form of text to data visualizations may seem to be counterintuitive, but this chapter shows you that with the right application, text can be a powerful addition to any data visualization. The chapter also explores the notion of text analysis, because applying it to your data visualization may make the difference between displaying intelligent data and displaying useless data.

Making Text Useful

One of the easiest ways to add context to any data visualization is to add text on or around a given visualization. Although you have an infinite number of ways to do this, this chapter focuses on a few specific techniques that make the process simple.

Before you go crazy adding text to your visuals, however, you should adhere to certain rules to avoid cluttering your visuals:

- **Use as few words as possible.** Text added to any data visualization must be complementary. Space is usually very limited, so your goal is to explain your visual with as few words as possible. E-mail marketers do this all the time, sometimes spending hours or even days on a single subject line, hoping to gain the highest e-mail open rate possible. The open rate is calculated by expressing the number of e-mails opened as a percentage of total e-mails.

  This process usually requires careful word choices, consideration of the limited space available in a single line, and multiple split tests to confirm the effectiveness of the chosen subject line. Done correctly, the process can increase e-mail open rates astronomically. The same is true of adding a line or two of text to a given data visualization. Done correctly, it can virtually eliminate misinterpretation of the data.

  Split testing is a marketing method that splits e-mail subscribers into two groups. Each group is sent a separate e-mail that is then tracked and compared based on specific metrics. The one with the better metrics is used.

- **Stick to simple words or single characters.** Using simple words is the key to providing your users an at-a-glance understanding of your visual and accompanying text. Say that a number has "gone up" or use an up arrow (↑) instead of saying that something has "increased," or say that something is "bad" rather than "negative." These examples present information in a way that's easy for anyone to digest.

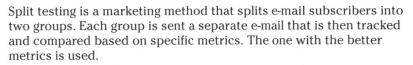

  Simplicity is key when it comes to choosing words.

Avoid using acronyms that require some existing knowledge or additional action to interpret.

✔ **Use single lines of text.** Besides keeping text simple, you need to keep it short. Just the sight of multiple lines of text may make a user hesitant to start reading that text. Your goal should be to use a single line of text that's easy to read and interpret.

✔ **Apply color sparingly.** Although adding RAG (red, amber, and green) alert colors can be useful, adding random colors to make text stand out against your visuals isn't a good idea. In general, data visualizations are color-rich, and adding text in a color that contrasts with the visual causes the text to compete with the visual. When you're a beginner, try to stick to text colors such as black, blue, and gray. Read more about using color in Chapter 10.

Colors are used as alert colors in data visualizations. Think of a traffic light: Red means "Stop, something is wrong!"; yellow means "Proceed, but with caution!"; and green means "Go, everything is OK!."

✔ **Know your data.** One cardinal rule about adding any form of text to describe a visualization is to make sure that the text applies to *every* scenario of the data being displayed — especially if the data is dynamic. This means that you can't include a static set of text for only one scenario of the data visualization, because the text won't be applicable when the data changes along with the scenario. This situation is where dynamic text comes in handy. You can read more about dynamic text in "Exploring Text Analysis," later in this chapter.

Now that you know the five main rules for adding text to data visualizations, it's time to explore a few techniques for applying those rules effectively.

Adding text labeling

The quickest way to apply text to any data visualization is to add labels. Labels describe what the user is seeing. They're easy to use, easy to read, and easy to apply.

Table 5-1 lists three types of text labels that you can add to any data visualization.

Table 5-1	Text Label Types
Label Type	**Description**
Title	Usually placed at the top of, inside, or alongside a specific visual. The title describes what the visual is displaying — Economic Growth in 2012, for example. Some higher-level titles may describe a section that includes multiple visuals.
Description	Normally located alongside or below a specific visual. These labels use a single word, text fragment, or sentence to describe the behavior of the visual. A good description sums up the message of any data scenario in a single sentence.
Value	May include a single number, letter, or combination of both in or on a given visual. The label usually stands alone or refers to a specific part of the visualization. A single visualization may have multiple values.

Most good data visualizations include all three types of labels.

Labels should be strategically positioned (see the next section), sized, and worded so that the text complements the visuals without overshadowing them. Going overboard with text can lead to something your users will see as just another report with some visuals.

Considering text positioning

You may have heard the saying "It's all about where you place it," which could not be truer when it comes to adding text to data visualizations. Wrongly placed text can lead to misinterpretation of the data.

You should follow two best practices in placing text on your data visualizations:

  ✔ **Keep all text horizontal.** Nonhorizontal text may confuse some of your potential users. We strongly advise that you stay away from positioning your text vertically or diagonally. Never force a user to tilt "his" or "her" head to read something! Stick to the basics by keeping all text horizontal.

Keep in mind that text is included to complement the visual, not overshadow or complicate it.

- **Keep all text within range of the visual.** The human eye naturally associates any text within a few centimeters of it as being related to it. In general, ensure that all text is within the range of the visual it's related to, because positioning text too far from the targeted visual can lead to confusion.

Figure 5-2 shows two basic bar charts. Both charts have a title label (refer to Table 5-1, earlier in this chapter), which is one of the most intuitive and common uses of text in any data visualization. The chart on the left has an easy-to-read horizontal label; the chart on the right has the same label tilted. Do you have to tilt your head to read the chart on the right? That label might be mistaken for an axis label.

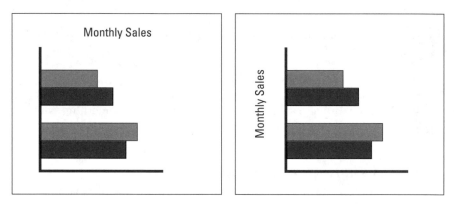

Easy-to-Read Title   Title may be mistaken for axis

Figure 5-2: A title is in two different places on these charts.

Choosing text fonts

Choosing the perfect text font for any given data visualization can be a tricky process. Although increasing the size of a word may convey emphasis or importance, it's not always the best route as it may overshadow the visuals.

Font sizes and formats

Here are some ideas to consider when you choose font sizes and formats:

- ✔ **Make important text a little bigger.** A general rule of thumb is that low-hierarchy text should be in a smaller font than high-hierarchy text. Figure 5-3 shows how the font sizes of various labels in a hierarchy may vary based on level.

This is a title...

This is a subtitle

This is the descriptive text and values.

Figure 5-3: Fonts vary in size based on level.

- ✔ **Consistency is key.** If you decide that all your main titles will be in a size 30 font, for example, you must ensure that all your main titles are exactly the same size.

  The key factor is to have consistency for each individual label type. Consistent label sizes for each level are easy for users to grasp, and the sizes help users identify certain areas of your data visualization at a glance.

- ✔ **Avoid using all caps.** The era of text messages and social media has created a new set of rules for using text. Today, using all caps indicates that someone is shouting, which usually evokes hostility and defensiveness. All caps are also harder to read, as all the letters are the same size. In addition, readers may gloss over or skip all-caps words.

  It may be fine to use a simple all-caps title such as SALES EXECUTIVE DASHBOARD, but don't use all caps in labels throughout your data visualization. In general, you have very little to gain from using all caps, so it's best to avoid the practice.

Font types

Thanks to web browsers such as Internet Explorer and Google Chrome, most people have become accustomed to a few standard fonts, such as Verdana, Garamond, Arial, Helvetica, and Times New Roman.

These fonts are somewhat boring, but we highly recommend sticking to one or more of them, for two reasons:

- **Each user's web browser may be different.** Data visualizations are commonly hosted on company sites or portals that must be viewed in a web browser (unless, of course, you're developing a static image like an infographic). No matter what fonts you use to create a data viz, each user's web browser automatically defaults displaying any text using one or more of the browser-safe fonts mentioned earlier.

  If you use unusual fonts, your visualization may look distorted or become unreadable when your fonts are replaced with browser-safe fonts. It's safer to design your visualization with the common fonts.

  One way to get around having to use browser-safe fonts is by posting your visualization in an Adobe PDF or Microsoft PowerPoint format. These file types are not affected by the browser, but these options are not available in all tools.

- **Avoid fancy or custom fonts.** Using fancy or custom fonts may make it harder for someone else to understand or edit your data viz, especially if you use nonstandard or specialized fonts that need to be individually downloaded and installed on a desktop. Yes, custom fonts may look great, but they are simply not worth the risk of having the user not being able to view them.

We recommend using Verdana and Garamond, both of which are on the extended list of browser-safe fonts. They add a little bit of flair without having the straight military feel of Arial.

Choosing text color

As we mentioned earlier in this chapter, you should choose a font color that's easy to read, such as black, gray, or dark blue. You should use this color scheme consistently throughout your data visualizations. The last thing you want is a bunch of color-rich visuals that are accompanied by colorful text; users would have a hard time deciphering what's important!

Consider a few guidelines when choosing text colors:

- **Consistency is king.** This won't be the last time we'll tell you to be consistent. Maintaining consistency of font color for specific label types is an absolute must. If you choose to put all descriptions in a dark gray color, then it's important that all descriptions receive this same treatment. Newbies often get the urge to change the color of particular text in an effort to bring more attention to it. They don't take into consideration how the change affects the entire data visualization. Avoid falling into the trap of using too many colors.

Avoid data overload

Mainstream advertisers often use the term *data overload* to scare the user community. Just type **data overload** in a search engine, and you'll see a series of data visualization software choices that are guaranteed to help even the most novice of users avoid the dreaded data overload syndrome by supposedly automating the generation of "useful" data visualizations! This promise is often an advertising ploy, though, so it's very important not to fall for this marketing trap.

A good rule of thumb is to ensure that your text-to-visuals ratio is 1:5, which means that you limit the use of text to roughly 20 percent of your overall data visualization. This ratio is a surefire way to ensure that you add value rather than clutter to your data viz.

✔ **RAG colors are sacred.** The use of red, amber, and green in all data visualizations is sacred, especially in the financial world. When it comes to data visualizations, these colors are automatically interpreted as meaning that something has gone wrong (red), something is about to go wrong (yellow), and everything is fine (green). These alert colors are used in data visualizations to provide notification when a measurement is heading to a good or bad status. When it comes to text, you should use only RAG colors to indicate alerts.

✔ **Bright colors are hard to read.** What happens when you see a neon-colored sign? It definitely captures your attention at first. But imagine having to look at the same sign every day! After a short period, you find that the sign isn't as easy to look at as it was when it first caught your attention. For this reason, avoid using bright-colored text in your data visualizations. Over time, muted colors will prove to be much easier for your users to read.

In some situations, however, a specialized color is required. See Chapter 10 for more information about those situations, which occur at a later stage in your data visualization journey.

Exploring Text Analysis

One of the most powerful ways to add context to your data visualizations is to include text analysis. In the Business Intelligence Dashboard Formula world (BIDF; see Chapter 1), text analysis is defined as a short sentence or fragment that contains a combination of static text and dynamic values that describe one or more visualizations.

Figure 5-4 shows a simple text analysis. The underlined words are *dynamic,* which means that they change based on the behavior of the data.

Sample Text Analysis Statement

ALERT: Expenses **have exceeded** monthly budget by **37%!**

Figure 5-4: Chart with text analysis statement with both static and dynamic text (underlined) that changes with the data.

Think of text analysis as being a real-time description of what's happening with the data. As the data changes, so does the descriptor. The trick is to create a statement that's smart enough to suit all scenarios of the data as it changes. Let's take a closer look at Figure 5-4 and how we built it.

First, you must know the data, as we mentioned earlier when we suggested rules you should follow for producing uncluttered visuals. For instance, in the example in Figure 5-4, we know that the chart is displaying expenses on a monthly basis. Therefore we establish the static parts of our sentence:

(ALERT): Expenses (dynamic text #1) monthly budget by (dynamic text #2).

Next you establish all the possible scenarios of the dynamic text (marked as blanks in the preceding example). In the case of Figure 5-4, we know that the possibilities for dynamic text #1 are that the expenses can exceed, not change, or remain below the monthly budget. Hence this sentence could have three different scenarios:

- **Scenario #1:** ALERT: Expenses (have exceeded) monthly budget by (dynamic text #2).
- **Scenario #2:** ALERT: Expenses (have not changed) monthly budget by (dynamic text #2).
- **Scenario #3:** ALERT: Expenses (remain below) monthly budget by (dynamic text #2).

Lastly, we need to fill in dynamic text #2. To calculate that rate for scenarios 1 and 3, we do a simple formula to find out by what percentage the expenses exceed or are below the budget.

Be sure to note the importance of not only covering all scenarios of the data but also changing the wording as needed to ensure the sentence makes sense. This is obviously a simple example, but it's a great place to start!

Determining what makes text analysis so important

When they first view a data visualization, most users do a two-part analysis. At first glance, they scan the visuals to get a sense of how the measurement is performing. Then, if time permits, they take a closer look at each visual to try to interpret what they're seeing. Their brains do a series of scans, capturing numbers, words, and colors to gain a clear idea of the message that the data is conveying.

You can use text analysis to eliminate this two-part process, however, by providing users with everything that they need to know in a single glance.

Text analysis serves two important purposes:

- **It prevents misinterpretation.** If 50 people see a single visualization, chances are that none of them will interpret the visualization exactly the same way. By providing text analysis, you essentially help users interpret the visualization clearly and make informed decisions.

- **It saves time.** Providing a clear, text-based interpretation of what a visual portrays saves users time, because they no longer have to stare closely at the visualization to gain a deeper understanding of the data.

Building a text analysis statement

How do you build a text analysis statement? Over the years, we've broken down thousands of text analysis statements and discovered that most of them contain the same four elements:

- **What:** This element refers to what you're actually measuring and usually is some form of key performance indicator or metric. Sales, expenses, margin, performance, and retention are all examples of measurements that you include at the beginning of your statement to let the user know what you're referring to.

✓ **What happened:** This element describes the behavior of the metric and uses measurement terms such as *high, low, up, down, increasing,* or *decreasing.* This behavior can also be represented with symbols, such as arrows.

✓ **By how much:** This element describes the magnitude of change in some numerical value.

Gauging the magnitude of any change is one of the best use cases for text analysis.

✓ **When:** A good guideline (when possible) is to include some reference to a time period to enable the user to gauge the effect of the change.

Figure 5-5 shows two simple text analysis statements that describe the same chart. Notice that the underlined dynamic words change as the data in the chart changes.

Positive Text Analysis

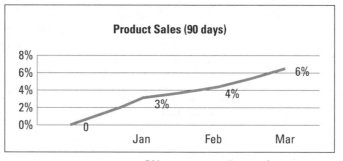

Sales went <u>up</u> by <u>6%</u> over the last <u>3 months</u>.

Negative Text Analysis

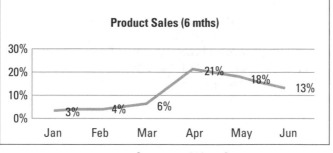

Sales went <u>down</u> to <u>13%</u> in <u>June.</u>

Figure 5-5: Examples of positive and negative opinions.

Incorporating dynamic text analysis into your data visualization makes your data truly intelligent. Including dynamic text analysis is low-hanging fruit with regard to your return on investment. It's easy to do and will delight your users. Some users may even think that you have magical data visualization powers!

Paying Attention to Detail

In This Chapter

▶ Knowing how people see design

▶ Communicating with pattern layouts

▶ Selecting a template

▶ Designing for different devices

*T*his chapter examines the way that people see and digest information. If you familiarize yourself with the common design conventions described in this chapter, you'll find it easier to create powerful visualizations that contain intelligent (actionable) data. In this chapter we look at principles that make up what is called "Gestalt" theory. It defines how what we see is translated into meaning. All the actions required to make meaning of things happens in our brains when we view things based on size and position.

This chapter also discusses the specific patterns that people use when viewing information. If you are aware of these patterns, you can more effectively structure your information. In addition, you see how to use a template to build on the knowledge of designers who have already thought through the issues you are facing as you build your data viz. Finally you look at the issues involved in designing for mobile devices and how that relates to the creation of your data viz.

Uncovering How People Digest Data

Recent advances in cognitive science have made it possible to scan the human brain and understand what happens when people view something. Researchers have learned more about the brain in the past ten years than they did in the previous hundred, which has made it possible to analyze brain function in exciting new ways.

Think about how we see. Our eyes gather information in small chunks, for example, even though we think we're seeing everything as a whole. When you're reading, your eyes take in several words, your brain makes mental pictures, and then your eyes move on to the next chunk of text. This process happens so quickly that you're unaware of it.

You may think that web designers create user experiences based solely on intuition and imagination. But believe it or not, today's designers adhere to Gestalt theory, which are principles uncovered by German psychologists in the early 20th century.

Gestalt means *unified whole* in English and is generally associated with the idea that the whole is greater than the sum of its parts. Gestalt theory is made up of several principles — including the concepts of proximity, similarity, closure, continuation, and figure/ground — that describe how the human brain sees visual information. Designers who understand this theory can develop visuals that communicate information in the most effective ways. We discuss each of these principles in turn.

Gestalt theory guides good designers when they create visualizations. You should also use the theory when you design your own data viz. You'll probably be surprised to find that you intuitively know the principles of Gestalt theory, which makes them even more powerful.

Here's how each principle influences what people see:

- **Proximity:** When items are placed in close proximity, people assume that they're in the same group because they're close to one another and apart from other groups. Figure 6-1 shows a visualization that includes grouped items. You can see the original image at `www.socialnomics.net/2012/10/16/state-of-social-marketing-survey-infographic`.

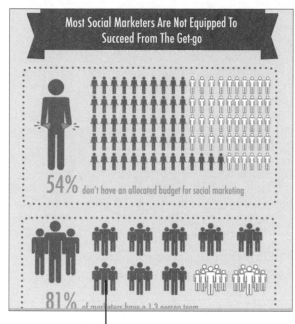

Grouped together

Figure 6-1: Items placed close together form a group.

- **Similarity:** When items look the same, people perceive them to be of the same type. We naturally assume that shapes that look the same are related. When you create a data viz and you keep items together that look the same, you make it easy for someone to understand that those items represent a group.

- **Closure:** Our eyes tend to add any missing pieces of a familiar shape. If two sections are taken out of a circle, as shown in Figure 6-2, people still perceive the whole circle.

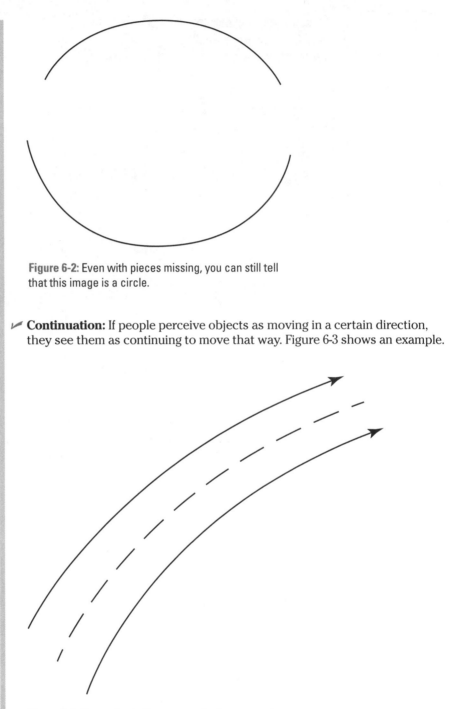

Figure 6-2: Even with pieces missing, you can still tell that this image is a circle.

✔ **Continuation:** If people perceive objects as moving in a certain direction, they see them as continuing to move that way. Figure 6-3 shows an example.

Figure 6-3: Items stay in the same path of movement.

✔ **Figure/ground:** Depending on how people look at a picture, they see either the *figure* (foreground) or the *ground* (background) as standing out, as shown in Figure 6-4.

Figure 6-4: Both the figure and the ground form shapes.

Presenting Common Visual Patterns

When you begin to create visualizations, you may be concerned about the placement of your charts, graphs, and other key data. Because you are new to data visualization, you may feel that you don't have accumulated knowledge about what works and what doesn't. Some reasons you may feel concerned include the following:

✔ You aren't sure about the placement of each element in the chart.

✔ You aren't clear about who your users will be for the data viz.

✔ You don't know where to put your menu items so they will be seen.

Fortunately, cognitive scientists have determined that people read text and images in certain specific patterns. As you organize the information in your visualization, using these standard patterns helps your users to scan the information quickly and easily.

Z and F patterns

Here are the two most common visual patterns:

- **Z pattern:** The Z pattern is often used for text and visual layouts. As you would expect, when a person's eyes follow the Z pattern, his eyes track from left to right across the top, down to the left, and then across the page at the bottom. Figure 6-5 shows the points of the Z numbered in the order in which the reader's eyes track across information on a page.

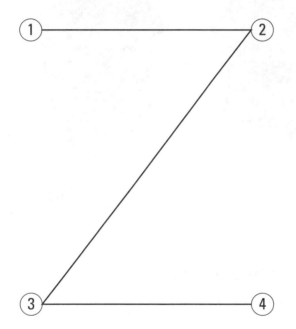

Figure 6-5: The Z pattern.

How does this pattern affect the layout of your content in a visualization? Your reader will scan the content along the path of the Z, so you should place the title at the top of the Z, along with any key content. Position more visual content in the middle and along the bottom.

- **F pattern:** Cognitive scientists have created heat maps to determine where the human eye goes when it looks at a web page. As shown in Figure 6-6, heat maps are composed of concentrations of colors that show where readers scanned the page. The most intense colors (red and yellow) show where readers' eyes lingered longest; readers spent less time looking at the blue areas. As you can see, the red and yellow areas resemble an F. You can see the original image at `http://doughayassoc.com/wp-content/uploads/2010/10/eyetracking_F-page.png`.

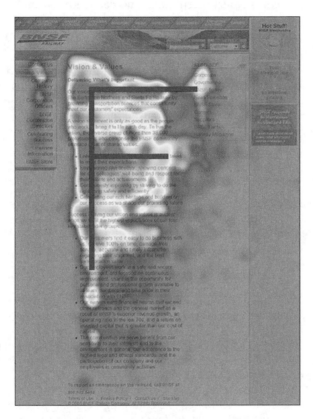

Figure 6-6: The F pattern on a heat map.

If you stick to these two layout patterns at the beginning, you can't go too far afield when designing your data viz.

Pattern design

Here are a few guidelines for using your knowledge of visual patterns to create a well-designed visualization:

- **Balance:** When you place items in your visualization, be sure to maintain balance. When too many items are clustered together, it's difficult for people to see how those items are related.

- **Color:** Random use of colors such as red can be misleading, causing the viewer to see an alert when there's no cause for alarm. Read Chapter 10 for more about using color in your visualizations.

- **Hierarchy:** You're familiar with the use of hierarchy as it pertains to a text outline. The top level of the outline may have a Roman numeral, the next level may have a capital letter, and then the third level may have a number. In a visualization, you can tell based on size or position which items are higher or lower on the hierarchy. You don't need to use numbering as you do in a written outline.

- **Repetition:** Repetition helps people become familiar with the items in a design. If you use the same elements throughout, people see a unified whole and don't have to guess what certain elements mean because they've seen those elements before.

- **White space:** The use of white space has been championed for decades. White space allows content to "breathe" — that is, your image benefits from ample space around the objects in the visualization. Too much clutter makes it hard for people to take in the image at a glance.

Deciding to Use a Template

Templates have become popular because they help novice designers use the expertise of more experienced designers. A template is a guide that helps you to create something using a model designed by others.

Many people feel that templates are confining because you have to place the objects in the spot that's been designated for them. In reality, though, templates are freeing, because they ensure that you create a balanced layout but still allow you to add your own look and feel. Here are some other benefits of templates:

- **Quick start:** Rather than sitting and puzzling over where to place your charts, numbers, and objects, you can begin to place those objects as designated by your template.

- **Expert design:** A template lets you draw on the skills of trained experts, which is a benefit if you're not a designer (and sometimes even if you are). There's clearly no downside to following the advice of people who are more skilled in an area than you are.

- **Cost savings:** Using a template enables you to forgo the services of a designer (although you may want to use a designer for complex projects).

Where less is more

Throughout this chapter, we talk about ways to incorporate design to make visualizations better. Restrictions can be good ways to improve your design. Think about how you're limited by space, for example. When you know that you can put only a few items in a data viz, you're forced to think harder about what is necessary.

Other design concepts follow the idea that less is more. Too many colors or typefaces are distracting, for example. Many designers like to limit the use of typefaces to two. Being familiar with design guidelines can help you avoid having a design that closely resembles a ransom note.

You can find templates for infographics and data viz wireframes in online tools such as Piktochart (http://piktochart.com) and Balsamiq Mockups (http://balsamiq.com).

See Chapter 8 for more information about using templates.

Achieving Consistency across Devices

As the popularity of mobile devices has increased, designers have had to face two new design issues:

- ✔ Design of mobile device interfaces
- ✔ Creation of apps for mobile devices

Until a few years ago, when a designer created a paper-based ad or brochure, she could plan exactly how it would look after it was printed. The designer knew the format and how customers would view it.

With the advent of the Internet, online designers used the few web browsers that were available to plan how their designs would look onscreen. The available tools were somewhat crude, but design was pretty straightforward. If he tested each web browser, a designer could determine what he needed to fix so the design would look right online.

Now designers have to design for a host of mobile devices, each of which has its own quirky needs. Consequently, the complexities of designing visualizations have grown.

Embracing responsive design

To deal with the issue of multiple screen sizes and operating systems, designers use the principle of *responsive design* (RD). RD refers to an interface or layout that can reconfigure itself based on where it's being viewed. The term was coined by Ethan Marcotte in a 2010 article (`http://alistapart.com/article/responsive-web-design`) that recognized the need for designers to address the issue of multiple screen requirements.

A website design that's responsive still looks good whether you view it on your desktop computer or on your smartphone. The rounded edges and icons that are common on smaller devices automatically fall into place.

In his article, Marcotte cited the three areas where RD can have the most effect in web design:

- **Fluid grids:** The grid is the tool that designers use to lay out their designs, regardless of whether those designs will be viewed online or offline. In Figure 6-7, a grid design has been transformed for three screen shapes. (You can find the original image at `http://searchengineland.com/figz/wp-content/seloads/2012/06/responsive-design-alone-not-mobile-seo.png`.)

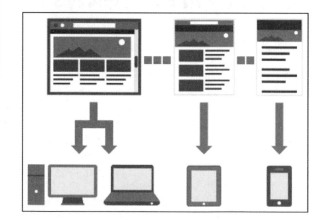

Figure 6-7: Grid design translated to different screens.

- **Flexible images:** When you have images in a blog post or on your website, you want to ensure that they're not cut off or distorted. Making sure that your images can reformat themselves is important.

- **Media queries:** When you enter a search term in a search engine such as Google or Bing, you want to be able to view the results on any of your screens. This is a key principle of RD. The content needs to be viewed on any mobile device a user might have. What makes viewing it on a variety of devices a challenge is that the designer has no way to know what the returned result will be.

These ideas apply to data visualizations as well. You want to make sure that your grid isn't distorted when the data viz is viewed on a mobile device. The images must be clear, and the aspect ratio (length to width) should be aligned regardless of the device the user is working with.

Following app design standards

Designers not only want an interface to look good but also want it to do all sorts of tricks. As a result, app design has become a discipline unto itself.

You may wonder why you should care about app design. Everyone who has to visualize anything online is subject to the same standards as any app designer.

In his article "Apple's 6 Simple Rules for Designing a Killer iOS App" (`http://mashable.com/2012/12/20/spun-ios-design`), Pete Pachal describes what he had to do to get his news app Spun certified for Apple's App Store. (At this writing, the app isn't available in the U.S. App Store.) Pachal's team had to work with Apple for five months to get everything perfected. During that time, Pachal codified six rules for his team. We've singled out four of these rules that apply to data viz design:

- **Simplicity is strength.** This rule is probably the most important rule for data visualizations. The goal is to explain or uncover new information that can be used to develop insights. If you focus on too many data points, the story will be lost. If you're creating a dashboard, this rule is particularly important because each piece of data needs to support the whole. (As Gestalt theory says, the whole is greater than the sum of its parts. See "Uncovering How People Digest Data," earlier in this chapter, for more about this theory.)

- **Don't sacrifice quality for time.** This rule is important for data visualization. If you slap together a visualization that's hard to decipher or just plain sloppy, no one will want to use it. Take the time to develop something great, and continue to refine it over time.

- **Reward the user with every touch.** Every menu item should do something useful. The print link should work, for example. Also, every click should provide information.

- **Details matter.** Before the user clicks a link in a data visualization, it should be apparent where that link will take her or what type of data she'll see.

Part III
Building Your First Data Visualization

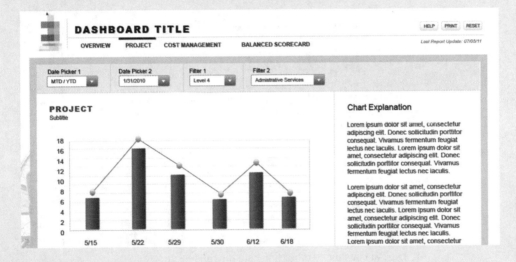

Visit www.dummies.com/extras/datavisualization to check out information on our handy BIDF Blueprint that you can use when you're creating your data viz.

In this part. . .

- ✔ Become familiar with Mico's easy-to-follow storyboard formula, which is called the Business Intelligence Dashboard Formula (BIDF).

- ✔ Find out how to develop a clear mock-up using the formula so that you avoid wasting time and money.

- ✔ See how to select and use effective visuals for your mock-up.

- ✔ Get familiar with the type of functionality and color you can add to your data viz.

- ✔ Look at how to add other finishing touches — such as effective navigation menus and navigational icons — to your data viz.

7

Defining an Easy-to-Follow Storyboard

In This Chapter

▶ Business Intelligence Overview

▶ Identifying your audience

▶ Defining your goals

▶ Documenting your metrics

▶ Choosing what to build

▶ Developing your first storyboard

*W*hen you're applying data visualization to Big Data, storytelling is perhaps one of the easiest ways to engage your audience. As social media continues to evolve, attention spans continue to reduce from minutes to seconds. As a result, complex reports and visualizations that require lots of deep analysis are losing their relevance. Hence, it's critical that you develop the "correct" story.

This chapter provides an overview of the practice of using data visualizations to drive decision making and then covers all the steps to defining your first storyboard. We start with identifying the audience, documenting their key measures, and then finally putting those measure into a visual storyboard. Defining an easy-to-follow storyboard requires some homework, and this chapter shows you how to work through a series of steps using a proven methodology and templates.

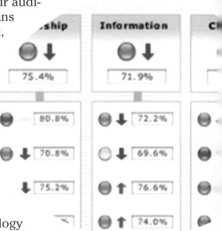

Business Intelligence Overview

Did you know that there is an entire multi-billion-dollar industry that focuses on the practice of building and using analytics reports and data visualizations (usually referred to as dashboards) to drive the decision-making process in large and small organizations? It's called Business Intelligence (BI). BI involves creating any type of data visualization (report, dashboard, or infographic) that provides insight into a business for the purpose of making a decision or taking an action.

Many people who are reading this book have been in the BI industry for many years without even realizing it. Whether you've been consuming some type of data for professional or personal use or building a report, dashboard, or infographic for others to use to make decisions, you've been part of the BI industry.

Now that you're clear on the definition of BI, you're probably wondering why BI is so important, especially if you're not familiar with it. There are two reasons why business intelligence should be important to anyone in the data visualization arena:

- ✔ **BI drives industry trends.** Trends in BI influence trends in many other areas, such as Big Data, mobility, social collaboration, and the cloud. These trends affect you as a data visualization consumer or creator, so it's important that you stay abreast of trends in the BI industry.

  If you're a consumer, for example, the rise of mobile and social collaboration determines where you access data visualizations, how you interact with them, and how you gain deeper insights from them.

- ✔ **BI drives the evolution of data visualization tools.** The BI industry is very competitive, and chances are that any tool you choose for building your data visualization will be classified as a BI tool. On one hand, this competition among different software vendors to build the ultimate tool works to everyone's benefit. It drives innovation that focuses on ease-of-use, better insight, and lower cost.

  On the other hand, the choice of tools is becoming so extensive that it's sometimes hard to decide on the best tool for the job. Consider the most widely used BI tool in the world: Microsoft Excel. Some members of the BI industry suggest that Excel, despite its wide adoption, is the most dangerous and least effective tool available. It's important to understand that the evolution of new software in this industry directly affects what types of tools are available to you.

After you have selected the right BI tools, it's time to develop a storyboard that will help you display the data. Throughout the rest of the chapter, we discuss the steps you need to take to set up your storyboard.

Delving Into Your Story

The most important step in building any data visualization is developing an easy-to-follow storyboard. In the BI community, storyboarding has a broad range of definitions.

For the purposes of this book, we use the Business Intelligence Dashboard Formula (BIDF) definition of storyboarding to keep it simple. This formula defines storyboarding as the act of translating user requirements into a four-part diagram that states the goal, measurements, and data visualization types. Using the BIDF storyboard, as shown in Figure 7-1, you can easily document each section discussed in this chapter to develop your story.

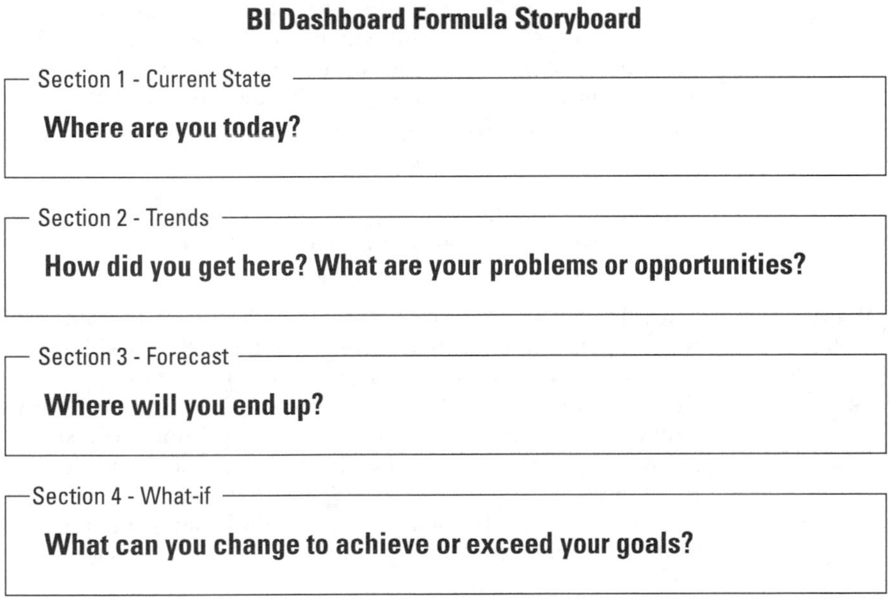

BI Dashboard Formula Storyboard

Section 1 - Current State

Where are you today?

Section 2 - Trends

How did you get here? What are your problems or opportunities?

Section 3 - Forecast

Where will you end up?

Section 4 - What-if

What can you change to achieve or exceed your goals?

Figure 7-1: BIDF storyboard sections.

The four main sections are

- **Current State:** Where are you now?
- **Trends:** How did you get here,?
- **Forecast:** Where will you end up?
- **What-if:** What can you change to achieve or exceed your goals?

Uncovering storyboard content

Before creating your first storyboard, you must decide what will be in it. If you focus on creating an easy-to-follow storyboard composed of actionable, intelligent data that outlines a clear story, building your final data visualization is fairly simple. First, you need to identify and document some key elements of your story by following these steps:

1. **Identify your audience.**

   Knowing your audience helps you quickly establish what kind of storyboard you're building and understand how to approach gathering the users' data and visual requirements.

   If your audience is comprised of C-level executives (such as the CEO, CFO, CIO, and so) or senior managers (such as vice presidents), you should expect them to have very little time to examine great detail. Your resulting data visualization and key performance indicators (KPIs) must be very high level, summarized views that give a 360-degree view of the company or specific area while allowing the user to drill down for further details.

2. **Document the audience's goals.**

   Gaining a clear understanding of your audience's goals and existing pain points will help you determine what to include and — more importantly — what not to include in the storyboard.

   Our BIDF team once worked with the president of a sales division who was responsible for annual revenue of more than $6 billion at one of the largest consumer-food-goods companies in the world. He explained to us that his goal was to drive his organization toward a sales level that would enable the sales team to receive their bonuses. He explained with great confidence, "If we can just get our sales team to do that, everything else will take care of itself." We immediately knew that our storyboard would have to focus on the year-end sales team bonuses; anything that didn't focus on helping the sales division hit its goal wouldn't appear in the storyboard.

3. **Define the audience's KPIs.**

   Understanding the key measurements that your audience must view, monitor, or track is the last step in developing your story. We recommend keeping your KPI count to fewer than 10 items combined because attention spans have gotten smaller, as has the average computer screen size!

   Our BIDF team once worked for a global telecommunications company that does about $10 billion in sales across the Caribbean and Latin America. The company identified almost 400 KPIs at the start of the project, and our team was admittedly a bit intimidated. Using the BIDF methodology discussed in this book, however, after two weeks and some late-night scoping sessions, we reduced the KPIs to fewer than 20.

Identifying your audience

The first step in developing a clear storyboard is identifying your audience. Who you're building your data visualization for ultimately determines what kind of storyboard you develop and what level of data you display.

The easiest way to classify your audience is to look at two simple components: line of business and job roles.

Line of business

Line of business (LOB) refers to an internal corporate business unit. The identified LOBs determine what kind of data to display. Human-resources data is very different from sales data, for example, in that it requires a lot of security and often the masking of sensitive employee data such as salary information.

Most big organizations have some of the following LOBs:

- Asset management
- Finance
- Human resources
- Information technology
- Manufacturing
- Marketing
- Procurement
- Research and development
- Engineering
- Sales
- Service
- Supply chain
- Sustainability

Although it's common to have multiple LOBs in a single storyboard, we recommend using a maximum of two *related* LOBs per storyboard.

The "one data visualization fits everyone" approach is a common pitfall for data visualization newbies, who often find themselves with an unused data-rich Picasso, as shown in Figure 7-2.

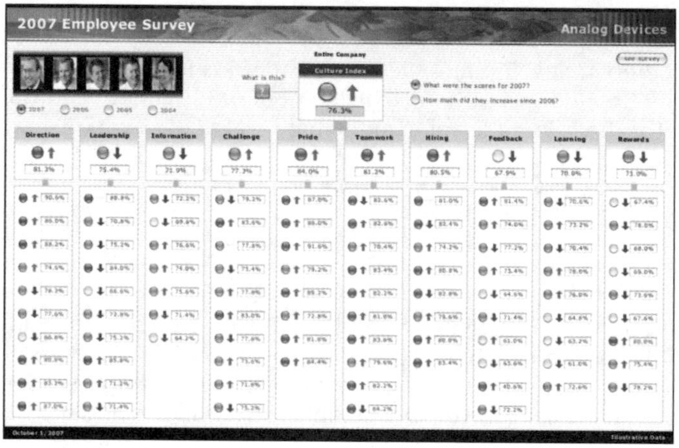

Figure 7-2: An example of an overdone visualization.

Job roles

This category refers to the role of a person or group of people in a given LOB and their stake in the resulting data visualization. The job titles and stakes of your audience members directly affect the level of data you should display in your data visualization.

Table 7-1 shows some of the most common job roles within an organization. Levels may vary by company size.

Table 7-1	Common Job Roles
Role	**Level of Data Display in Storyboard**
C-level (CEO, CIO, COO, CFO, and so on)	Company overview High-level data
Vice presidents and senior managers	Multi-division view High-level data
Supervisors and directors	Departmental view High-level data Drill down to details
Managers	Team view Drill down to details
Staff (individual contributors)	Operational view Drill down to details

Documenting Goals

Now that you've clearly established your audience type, you need to identify and document the audience's goals. The easiest way to do this may be to hold a small planning session that includes the executive sponsor (if there is one) and representatives of each job role in each LOB.

If the sales manager is requesting the data visualization, for example, it's important that you have that sales manager present, as well as one or two members of her reporting team to ensure that all parties agree on the identified goals. Although in-person meetings are preferable, most global organizations find it challenging to do planning sessions in person. We recommend requesting a simple conference call.

Avoid sending e-mails to accomplish this task. You'll only receive multiple, conflicting goals that take extensive time to track down and align with each job role.

Although goal gathering can appear to be a simple task, chances are that it will reveal conflicting agendas and priorities across different job roles. This is why it's critical to have the executive sponsor or most senior job role present to dictate and align the goal of the data visualization. If a senior-level sponsor is missing, your audience members may be confused and may distance themselves from the rest of the process. This scenario is your worst nightmare. Don't overlook this requirement.

To guide the goal-gathering process, ask each person present the following two questions, and be sure to document their individual answers:

✔ **What are your problems and pain points today?**

Ask the audience members to focus on problems that can be fixed with a resolution that can be measured quantitatively. Here are examples of quantifiable and nonquantifiable problems:

- *Quantifiable problem:* If the sales manager states that sales are declining because too much money is being spent on old marketing campaigns that aren't producing results anymore, an opportunity exists. You can review historical trends, identify declining campaigns, and reallocate the spending to boost high-performing marketing campaigns, thereby increasing sales.

- *Nonquantifiable problem:* If the sales manager states that the sales have declined by 5 percent to 10 percent for the past four years due to a lack of motivation among the sales reps, you should avoid trying to measure this decline. Avoid statistical measurements that require heavy data modeling, such as regression and T-models.

✏ **What are your goals, and what does success look like?**

These questions usually invoke a wealth of responses. You want to be sure to get each goal down to a simple statement and keep the count to the top three or four most important goals.

In addition, the goals need to include quantifiable responses that can be measured with a defined target. Each goal should tie directly to solving one or more of the problems identified in the responses to the first question, which is the only way you'll be able to measure the return on investment of your Big Data visualization project.

Here are two examples that show you the difference between good and bad goals:

✏ **CFO (Chief Financial Officer):** "We want to increase our company's revenue by 10 percent in the next 12 months. This will require that we bring in an additional $500 million in revenue across all divisions."

We consider this to be a *good goal* because it has a clear target with a set timeframe that can be measured.

✏ **Sales Manager:** "We hope to influence when our product hits the sales shelves, to drastically improve our ability to sell more, and therefore to hit our target of a 10 percent revenue increase in the next 12 months. However, because we are distributors and have no actual control over the shelving process in the stores, our sales rep will be required to visit the store managers twice as much each month to build the relationships, hopefully influencing our products hitting the shelf sooner."

This is considered to be a *bad goal* because the sales manager is seeking to increase his revenue by reducing the time it takes for products to hit the shelf — an action that he today has no influence over. This is a typical case of users wanting to view data that is not intelligent (unactionable).

When you're able to document one to four solid goals, your aim is to gain consensus for each goal among the entire group to prevent confusion going forward.

Table 7-2 shows the answers that members of a sales team provided when they were asked to complete the BIDF Planning Guide.

As you can see, some of the problems listed in Table 7-2 refer to cultural issues and broken processes, which is common for most customers. This confirms the need for a data visualization that provides a single version of the truth.

Table 7-2	BIDF Planning Guide Sample
Questions Asked	*Responses*
What are your problems or pain points today?	Too many analytical touch points (users spending too much time building reports) Data hoarding by analysts prevents identifying new opportunities Conflicting sales priorities
What are your goals, and what does success look like?	Hit the target to receive bonuses Effectively manage campaign budget to increase profitability

The good news is that these goals are very quantitative. After you confirm the expected target, bonus, and increase in profitability for each person, you can create the storyboard easily. We discuss this topic more in the next chapter.

Documenting KPIs

After you've documented the high-level goals, you need to capture and document your audience's KPIs. In simple terms, a *KPI* is a core measurement that ties directly to the company's goals. In the sales-team example, the sales manager might identify revenue as a KPI, as it's critical that this number is tracked on a regular basis to ensure it will hit the company target.

Conducting scoping workshops

The best way to work with your audience to document their KPIs is to conduct a series of scoping workshops. These workshops can be done virtually or (preferably) in person, like the planning sessions.

For the purposes of this book, we use the BIDF definition of *scoping:* an event where a group of identified super users from each LOB gather (physically or remotely) to openly discuss and define their business requirements.

Although conducting these workshops may seem to be innocent, if not handled properly, they can quickly turn into a never-ending list of requirements that will never fit into a single data visualization.

After all of the KPIs are identified and documented, it's important to ask the following question about each one: Does this KPI help the user achieve one or more of the goals listed in the Planning Guide?

If the answer is yes, proceed to collect and document the next KPI. If the answer is no or undecided, question the relevance of the KPI to this data visualization project and try to discourage group members from putting any useless information in the data visualization.

A data visualization should tell a clear story. Like any story in the multimedia world, it should have a clear narrative that includes a plot (in this case, achieving goals).

We recommend using the BIDF BI Blueprint (which you can download online for free at `www.dummies.com/extras/datavisualization`), shown in Figure 7-3.

Purge KPIs			Execution - Key Metric Identification					Data Collection		Monitor				Status
Final	Available	Priority	P	Existing Report	Area	KPI	Hierarchy	Owner	Source	Viewing Period	Report Freq. Portal	Alerts	TurnOffs	as of 05/01/2013
Y or N	3 of them	J.2, Phase 3	1	SalesReport.xls	Sales, Marketing, Finance	Margin	Cost of Goods Sold	CFO	Out Module, Excel, Oracle, Oracle-x.2	TBD	Weekly, Monthly, Quarterly, Annually	1. G - > Yellow/ 2. Y- Over - >/ 3. G- > Red	HR Only	Data sheet submitted to Matt
			1	SalesReport.xls	Finance	Sales	Sales	CFO	SAP Sales Module					5/2/13 - John said it will be available on 5/31/10
			2	SalesReport.xls	Finance	Sales	Cost of Goods Sold							
			3	SalesReport.xls	Finance	Margin	Margin							

Figure 7-3: BIDF BI Blueprint.

Understanding the key measurements that must be viewed, monitored, or tracked by your audience members is a vital but tricky process. Most users want to see more data than they actually need to address their problems.

Identifying example KPIs

Table 7-3 shows some KPIs derived from the sales team in our continuing example.

Table 7-3	KPIs and Definitions
KPIs	**Definitions**
Sales	Expected revenue based on all customer transactions
Annual goal	Sales revenue target that determines bonus
Probability of hitting annual goal	Calculates the chances of the sales rep hitting their annual goal
Deductions	Expected revenue not paid by customer
Available trade spend	Amount of money available to use in customer promotions

The KPIs listed in Table 7-3 are well defined and include concise definitions that resonate with all the business users.

By now, you should have a clear idea of what your audience members need to see to accomplish their goals. Pat yourself on the back. At this stage, 40 percent of the heavy lifting is done. But before you can proceed to create a mock-up (the first-draft preview of your data viz), you need to choose what kind of data visualization to build.

Building Your First Storyboard

Although the concept of storyboarding isn't new, the approaches and tools available to create storyboards continue to evolve. Mico recalls building her first storyboards with pencil and paper or on whiteboards with dry-erase markers. Over time, she scanned and moved those sketches to Microsoft PowerPoint. Fortunately, a plethora of tools specifically geared to this task is available now.

This book uses the BIDF storyboard section for section outline shown in Figure 7-1, earlier in this chapter, to make the process easy to follow.

Section 1: Current State

Section 1: Current State of the storyboard describes the user's current state. It should answer two simple questions: What is the current status of the main goal(s)? What is the likelihood of hitting or missing the main goal(s)?

In the continuing sales example, the sales managers identified their overall goal as hitting their bonuses. Therefore, you determine that Section 1 should display the information shown in Figure 7-4.

BI Dashboard Formula Storyboard

Section 1 - Current State

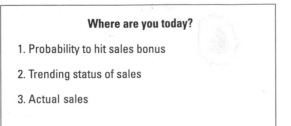

Where are you today?

1. Probability to hit sales bonus

2. Trending status of sales

3. Actual sales

Figure 7-4: Sales Storyboard Example Section 1: Current State.

Time is relative to the actual KPI. "Where you are now?" could mean today, yesterday, last quarter, or last year. It really is based on how it makes sense to measure that goal.

In the sales storyboard example, you're tracking whether the sales team will hit its bonuses. So your main KPIs would be

- **Probability to hit sales bonus:** Likelihood of the sales reps actually getting their bonuses
- **Trending status of sales:** Comparison of behavior of sales over a specified period
- **Actual sales:** Current sales amount

Although the data is being updated and viewed on a daily basis, it's being tracked on a monthly and yearly basis to keep track of the long-term goal. Bonuses are paid at year-end, but viewing them on a monthly basis breaks the tasks into smaller, achievable milestones, which makes it more digestible for the user.

When developing the KPIs for this section and all other sections, it's important to focus on the behavior of your typical user, who is likely to have less than a minute to scan his or her status before a big meeting. This section should let the user see at a glance whether things are going well or badly.

Section 2: Trends

Section 2: Trends of the storyboard describes how the user got to the current state. For example, if the current state shows that the main goal is off target, then the trends area should display a set of measurements that show exactly what factors contributed to missing the target. Conversely, if the current state shows that the main goal is on or above target, then the trends area should display a set of measurements that shows the factors that contributed to this success.

The description of the measurements that will be shown in the sales storyboard is shown in Figure 7-5. Assume that the probability of the manager hitting his goal is low. Your next step is to work with the users to determine the top reasons why sales managers may or may not hit their goals and the effect of those measurements on the overall goal.

BI Dashboard Formula Storyboard

Section 2 - Trends

How did you get here?

1. Marketing campaigns (show 12 months of ROI variance, mark highest negative variances)

2. Unshipped items (show dollar amounts)

3. Customer missed targets (show top 5 highest missed customer sales targets MTD)

4. Speed to shelf (show retailers with most delayed speed-to-shelf times)

Figure 7-5: Sales Storyboard Example Section 2: Trends.

Following are some of the top reasons that the main sales goal may be missing its target, which you might derive after talking with the users and studying some of the data from their existing reports:

- ✔ **Marketing-campaign performance:** Money spent on a given marketing campaign versus the ROI (return on investment) received is low.

- ✔ **Unshipped items:** Items expected to be shipped on a given date are not shipped, leading to a loss in sales.

- ✔ **Customer missed sales targets:** Projected sales targets for given retail customer(s) has not been met.

- ✔ **Speed to shelf:** The time it takes a retailer to place items on the shelf (can't be influenced by a sales manager) is delayed, resulting in a loss in sales.

There are always going to be a host of reasons why a goal is not being met. The idea is to focus on the 20 percent of the reasons that are resulting in 80 percent of the failure.

Focus on metrics that are within the user's control, as data visualizations need to contain actionable data. Displaying information that isn't actionable is a waste of the user's time and leads to low user adoption. In the example, the speed-to-shelf measure, for instance, is one that should be questioned.

Don't display data just for the sake of displaying it — a common mistake among data visualization newbies.

To ensure that the user understands why you're displaying these particular measures, show the cumulative and individual impact of each measure on the overall sales goal.

This is why you don't want to have low-impact or nonactionable measurements. If users can't immediately gauge the importance of the measurements as a part of the story, you lose their attention. Worse, users may proceed to do their own analysis, which defeats the purpose of providing useful information in your data visualization.

Section 3: Forecast

Section 3: Forecast of the storyboard should provide a clear projection of where the main sales goal will end up if no action is taken. It should also provide a clear view of where the main goal will end up compared with the original target and highlight any gaps.

For the sales storyboard example, you can use the metrics from Section 2: Trends of the storyboard, this time highlighting future behavior and effect on the existing goal:

- **Sales forecast:** Projections of sales figures for the next 12 months based on existing trends

- **Marketing-campaign performance:** Projection of performance for rest of month based on existing trend

Figure 7-6 shows what Section 3: Forecast of the storyboard might look like.

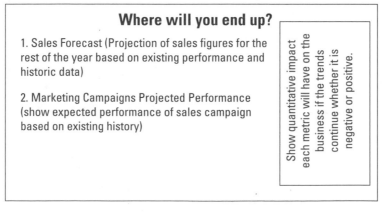

Figure 7-6: Sales Storyboard Example Section 3: Forecast.

Just like all elements of your storyboard, the forecast referred to in this book has to be actionable. It should either encourage the actions described in Section 4: What-if of the storyboard (the what-if section) or discourage the actions of the user that have led to the current outcome.

Section 1: Current State of the storyboard (refer to Figure 7-4) displays sales versus target, sometimes confused with the forecast. Therefore, including the same information in Section 3: Forecast would be repetitive. To continue the story, simply display a projection of the metrics from Section 2: Trends of the storyboard.

After the correct list of measurements has been established, it's sometimes easier to display the forecast as a function of the current state or trends section. Not only is real estate of most data visualizations very limited, but including the forecast as a simple line on a chart or number display next to the KPI helps to effectively get the point across in most cases.

Section 4: What-if

The way we approach this section in the BIDF world is very different from traditional BI practice, and it truly delivers value when you're developing a Big Data visualization.

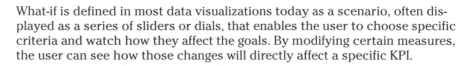

What-if is defined in most data visualizations today as a scenario, often displayed as a series of sliders or dials, that enables the user to choose specific criteria and watch how they affect the goals. By modifying certain measures, the user can see how those changes will directly affect a specific KPI.

We assume that you're reading this book because you truly want to provide insight into your organization's Big Data. You want to avoid just placing charts on a sheet and calling the sheet a data visualization. We also assume that you're actually trying to develop something that folks might view as being highly intelligent.

Now that we're on the same page, let us repeat that truly valuable Big Data visualizations focus on providing intelligent actionable data to users. Providing a set of sliders on the data viz that let users go on a wild goose hunt for the ultimate scenario is a waste of their time. When that happens, users will abandon the data viz for something that provides the answer so that they don't have to find the ideal scenario through trial and error.

The what-if section of your BIDF storyboard provides the missing piece of the story: a clear set of recommendations that, if followed, will help the users improve their current state. You provide the most optimal combinations of actions the users can take to have the greatest effect on achieving their goals.

Suppose that the sales manager isn't meeting her goal. From the trends, we already know what happened. In Section 4 we want to display some suggestions for improving the current situation. The suggestion may look like this:

- **Bad marketing-campaign performance:** Money spent on a given marketing campaign(s) didn't provide the expected return in sales.

  Based on the available historic and existing data, an example recommendation may be to move money from the existing campaign to a campaign that has been performing consistently for the last 5 years, though with much lower returns.

- **Missed shipped items (dollars):** Items expected to ship on a given date either shipped late or not at all.

  Based on the available historic and existing data, an example recommendation may be to immediately source the product from a warehouse that is stocked and has historically shipped on time to avoid the loss in sales.

- **Top 3 unmet customer sales targets:** Sales targets with given retail customer(s) were lower than projected.

  Based on the available historic and existing data, an example recommendation may be to focus on a set of smaller customers who have a history of great sales to make up for the missed sales targets with the other customers.

One easy way to make these recommendations digestible to the user is to provide three buckets of options with different risk levels, as shown in Table 7-4.

Table 7-4	What-if Examples
What-if Buckets	*Recommendations*
Option A Risk Level – High Impact – 98%+	Reallocate 100% of Campaign A funding to Campaign B, which has been performing in a similar region. Launch a new campaign in the East Coast region based on previous-year sales at a specific store.
Option B Risk Level – Medium Impact – 87%+	Reduce funding of Campaign A to less than 70%. Add a discount to existing promotion to make it more attractive. Focus on three smaller customers who have a solid sales history to make up the two missed customer sales targets.
Option C Risk Level – Low Impact – 60%+	Reduce funding of Campaign A to less than 30%. Add an online coupon option to existing promotion. Re-allocate the order to Warehouse A, which is fully stocked and historically ships on time.

This example gives users several options with varying levels of risks and effect to contemplate. The system has already done the analysis that would otherwise be done manually in an Excel spreadsheet and provides a clear path for users to achieve their goal and ultimately achieve success.

Give yourself a pat on the back! The process that you just went through is perhaps the most difficult part of building any data visualization. It's essentially the blueprint by which you provide true intelligence.

The sales storyboard sums up the customer's sales story by letting the sales manager know

- Whether he's going to hit his goal
- How far he is from hitting or missing his goal
- What actions led to missing or hitting his goal (show the exact effect those trends had on the goal)
- Where he will end up if he continues down the same course (show the exact effect those trends will have on his goal)
- What actions he can take to hit or exceed his goal (show a list of actions, their risk factors, and how they will affect the goal)

Be excited. At this stage, your user is going to think you're a data visualization god!

8

Developing a Clear Mock-Up

In This Chapter

▶ Going from storyboard to mock-up

▶ Knowing when to use color

▶ Using a template

▶ Developing your first mock-up

*A*fter you've done the hard work of defining and outlining your story-board, it's time to develop your mock-up. Mock-ups are also referred to as *wireframes* or *prototypes*. Think of them as rough sketches that help you visualize what the final output will look like.

Much like developing your storyboard, developing a clear, effective mock-up requires working very closely with your users. This is where many newbies get into trouble. If the process isn't handled correctly, it can quickly turn into a never-ending cycle of layout and color changes.

You'll quickly discover that the Big Data visualization world is full of what we call "color-crazy users." They can become your worst nightmare unless you follow the proven, untraditional approach we use in the Business Intelligence Dashboard Formula (BIDF) described in this book.

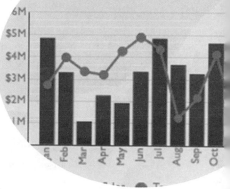

In this chapter, you discover how to start with a simple black-and-white sketch to focus your users on confirming your mock-up layout. In Chapter 9, you see how to apply effective visuals that convey your storyboard message. In Chapter 10, you discover how to add functionality and color to finalize your mock-up.

Getting Started with Your Mock-Up

Mico learned the hard way that working with users to develop anything visual is like handing candy to a baby. Without some guidance and hand-holding, users can't help but overindulge in color and chart changes. They lose focus and miss the opportunity to effectively display the story their data is trying to tell.

Mock-ups are particularly important in the Big Data visualization process for two reasons:

- ✔ **They help accelerate the overall design discussion and process with the users.** It's much easier to change a sketch of the data than it is to change the final model.

- ✔ **They help users understand the look, feel, and functionality of the final data visualization.** Mock-ups help to prevent any cosmetic surprises for the users when they see the final data visualization.

In the Big Data visualization world, visuals are made for data — not data for visualizations. This means that any design choice made based on the idea that it will be "sexy" often leads to a non-user-friendly visualization that doesn't convey the message of the storyboard effectively.

Sticking to black and white

You may find the title of this section a bit unexpected. After all, isn't one of the main points of data visualization to use elements like color to tell the most effective stories from the data? The answer is yes, but not during the mock-up stage.

If you start the mock-up process with color, your users won't focus on anything else — not on the data, on the layout, or even on whether the message is being conveyed correctly. The color discussion will become the focal point of the entire mock-up process, and your final data visualization will suffer.

Mico clearly remembers her first experience working with five color-crazy users at a Fortune 50 company. The discussion about the final shade of the colors for the alerts lasted days beyond the allotted project time. The resulting data visualization, which was late, was not worth showing.

Don't be perturbed if you have a similar experience. Sticking to black and white in initial mock-ups is the key to avoiding repeats of that experience. By using mock-ups without color, you force users to focus on what you need them to focus on.

Your only goal at this stage is to get participants to sign off on the layout of your mock-up. You don't need to do anything fancy or artsy to get that approval.

Although this approach seems to be fairly logical, we realize that some of you may be nervous about taking it. You may fear that users may grow impatient with or be turned off by a plain black-and-white mock-up. To overcome this worry, you should make it a habit to reiterate and set expectations up front about what users should expect to happen next and in the final outcome.

We always tell the users that color will be added as the last step, but we need them to focus on the layout before they can get to the fun stuff. This discussion is fairly easy to have, and most users won't object.

The exception to this rule is mock-ups created for an executive audience. Your time with executives is likely to be limited, so it's critical that you don't approach them until you have a fully functional, well-branded visualization (see Chapter 10). Anything less, and you risk being axed!

Some other benefits of sticking to black and white for your initial mock-up include the following:

- **Saves time and money when making changes:** It's less expensive to make design modifications on a black-and-white sketch than it is to make changes on a system-ready visualization connected to live data.

- **Keeps the focus on the placement, position, and size of each element on the visualization:** Laying things out in a flat, colorless space helps you figure out where to place each component to provide a nice, clear user interface that tells a compelling story. Color sometimes distorts your view of the overall layout and causes you to focus on the shiniest items in the model.

Now that you know why it's so important to stick to black and white for your mock-ups, we'll discuss the most effective tools to use.

Using good ol' pencil and paper

Although software is available for doing just about everything, including drawing your mock-ups, don't overlook the good old pencil-and-paper approach. It's as good now as it was in 1801, when the first pie chart appeared in William Playfair's publication *The Statistical Breviary*.

Figure 8-1 shows the most basic tools you can use to create a mock-up: papers and a pencil and an eraser.

Figure 8-1: Pencil and paper worked in the 1800's, and they still work today.

To get started, you should have some blank white paper (or a sketch pad of some sort), two pencils, and a big eraser. You'll be doing a lot of erasing.

As software continues to evolve, however, there are fewer arguments for using pencil and paper. Here are a few pros for the old-fashioned method:

- **Low cost:** A few sheets of white paper, a pack of pencils, and a big eraser will set you back $10 at most, although it's likely that you already have most of these items in your possession.

- **No learning curve:** You can just pick up a pencil and start drawing. You don't need to learn how to use a toolbar or menu options in software.

- **More creative freedom for newbies:** It would be great if we were all blessed with graphic design skills. We're sure that you'd love to know how to use advanced graphics tools like Adobe Photoshop to whip up any visualization you desire. But most of us have no formal design training and need to stick to the basics. Pencil and paper provide the freedom to be as creative as you want without being hampered by a key-board, mouse, or annoying pop-ups on the screen.

Here are a few arguments against using pencil and paper:

- **Sharing can be difficult.** You won't have convenient options for sharing your mock-up to collaborate with your users or get their feedback.

- **Paper pages are often too small to share with a large audience.** Even big sheets of paper may be hard for everyone to see at once.

✔ **Paper lacks security.** To ensure the highest level of security, most organizations encourage their employees to embrace a digital lifestyle. Doing nightly backups on employees' PCs enables the company to minimize the impact of a disaster. Having a paper trail with no backup is asking for an accident. Based on some embarrassing experiences, we've exchanged some of our pencil-and-paper habits for more web-based ones.

Using web-based or desktop tools

Although this market is still maturing, using a software-based tool to do your mock-up can be quite beneficial for several reasons:

✔ **It's easy to get feedback.** Collecting feedback on your mock-up is easy when you use online or web-based tools. Most applications provide multiple options that allow you to export mock-ups in the form of PDF or image files. You can send these files to your users electronically to get their feedback.

✔ **Inviting collaborators is simple on the web.** Knowledge sharing and collaboration are vital parts of the mock-up process. By hosting mock-ups on the web, you can invite co-workers and other team members to provide their input or feedback.

Be very careful about giving other people permission to modify your mock-ups directly. Not knowing who did what can lead to chaos.

✔ **You save time when making modifications.** The beauty of using software is that you can easily save old and new versions of your model for comparison purposes. Then it's easy to incorporate users' feedback and present updated mock-ups.

✔ **You can build a reusable library.** One much-overlooked benefit is the ability to create a library of template mock-ups that you can save and then reuse for future products. Templates save time, and it's much easier to start with a previous mock-up than it is to start with a blank canvas.

✔ **Most software tools are free or inexpensive.** Most tools on the market today are free to individual users for a specified number of mock-ups. If you want to invite more collaborators or have multiple projects running at the same time, the most sophisticated web tools cost anywhere from $5 to $100 per month for use by an entire team.

As the market for software that allows users to design prototypes rapidly continues to evolve, do an Internet search for *online mock-up tools* to get an updated list of software choices.

Discovering some software tools

Here are two of our top software choices.

Balsamiq Mockups

One of the best-known, most popular mock-up tools is Balsamiq Mockups (`http://balsamiq.com`), a cloud-based service (with an accompanying desktop application) that enables you to create fun and interactive website mock-ups quickly and easily. With its trademark sketchy, hand-drawn look, as shown in Figure 8-2, Balsamiq Mockups is currently our number-one choice for black-and-white mock-ups, and we like the fact that adding color or images is simple.

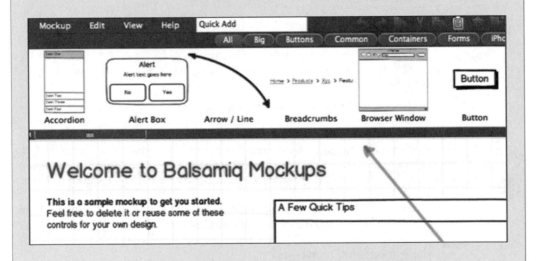

The application comes with a huge collection of drop-in components, reusable libraries, and an easy drag-and-drop interface. Because it's cross-platform and has full offline support, you can create mockups anywhere. At this writing, the desktop application starts at around $79 (one-time fee) for a single-user license. Plans start at $12 per month.

Mockup Tiger

Mockup Tiger (`www.mockuptiger.com`) is a web-based/desktop application that enables you to create dashboard mock-ups as shown in Figure 8-3 and share them with clients or co-workers.

Mockup Tiger comes with even more components than Balsamiq Mockups that can be used specifically for dashboarding. It includes an easy-to-use drag-and-drop interface.

When you're ready to share your mock-up, you can export projects as PDF or image files, or you can share them directly with others who have access to Mockup Tiger. People with access can leave feedback and comments on the project.

Building Template Layouts

Whether you've chosen to use pencil and paper or a software mock-up tool, the good news is that you don't need to reinvent the wheel. Building and using templates is the quickest and smartest way to approach designing your mock-ups.

The elements shown in Figure 8-2 make up your first mock-up template. Each element corresponds to one of the following steps:

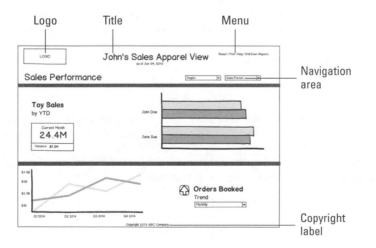

Figure 8-2: Elements of a mock-up.

1. **Start with a frame.**

   Start by drawing a simple, square frame. Think of this frame as being the home of all your data visualization elements.

2. **Determine where to place the logo.**

   Company branding is a top priority for most organizations. We recommend placing your logo in the top-right or top-left corner of your frame. Although some people argue that placement in the bottom-left corner of the frame works well, we prefer to place elements such as logos at the top.

3. **Add a title.**

   The title of your mock-up is very important and should be housed in the top-right corner or center of your frame. The title is the first thing that most users will see, and you want to make it very clear what they're viewing.

4. **Provide a help menu section.**

   You may want to include a set of help buttons in your data visualization. Some of the most popular options include

   - *Print button:* Allows users to print the data viz from their devices as needed

   - *Reset button:* Allows users to start from the beginning

   - *Help button:* Provides helpful information about the data viz

   - *FAQ button:* Provides information about various aspects of the data viz

5. **Add a navigation area.**

   The easiest way to tackle this section is to think about your three favorite websites. The navigation elements of those sites are probably along the top, on the left side, or in both places. Because users read in a backward Z pattern, these areas are the most effective places for any navigational menus.

6. **Add a copyright line.**

   This line usually goes at the bottom of the data visualization to ensure that users see that the work is copyrighted.

Now that you've included the main elements, it's time to decide on a layout to display your data elements, as shown in Figure 8-3.

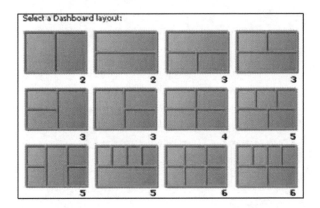

Figure 8-3: Choosing a layout.

 Your layout is the body of your mock-up, where the visualizations are housed. All the elements that we describe in Figure 8-2 are elements that surround the layout.

9

Adding Effective Visuals to Your Mock-Up

In This Chapter

▶ Examining common traits of effective visuals

▶ Creating insight and not hindsight

▶ Transitioning from storyboard to visual mock-up

*W*hen your black-and-white mock-up is complete, you're ready to add the oh-so-powerful visuals that will make it pop. That's why you started this journey to begin with, right? When adding visuals to your mock-up, it's important to focus on adding effective visuals. Unfortunately, due to a lack of thought leadership and training in the business intelligence (BI) industry, tons of visually attractive but ineffective data visualizations provide zero value. Just do an Internet search for *data visualizations* to see a few examples.

This chapter takes a closer look at what constitutes effective visuals. By way of comparison, it also looks at the qualities of some ineffective visuals.

Visuals are much more than just charts. As you can see from the topics covered in this book, great data visualizations are a combination of charts, objects, and text placed strategically to tell a story of the data.

Recognize the Three Traits of an Effective Visual

Table 9-1 lists the three main traits of an effective visual.

Table 9-1	Three Traits of an Effective Visual
Trait	*Details*
Data is clear	Make sure that the data is clear, both in purpose and display.
Visual fits the data	Whether you choose a chart or text, be sure that you're using the right visual for the job.
Exceptions are easy to spot	Whether you're highlighting a comparison or outliers in the data, you should make it easy for your users to identify exceptions in the data.

The preceding table was influenced by Edward Tufte, who is considered to be the godfather of data visualization. His book *The Visual Display of Quantitative Information,* 2nd Edition (Graphics Press), is one of the most highly regarded books in the data visualization field. Though it takes a scientific approach, it's a must-read for data viz beginners and experts alike.

The following sections provide more detail on the traits listed in Table 9-1.

These three traits aren't all-inclusive, so you shouldn't expect to have all of them to decide whether a visual should make it into your mock-up. Instead, use them as guidelines as you choose your visuals. The more traits you have in each visual, the more effective your overall data viz will be!

Data is clear

Effective visuals display data that's clear in both presentation and purpose, not distorted in any way. A common mistake is to push too much data into a single visual, causing the important point of the data to be hidden, overshadowed, or distorted by all the noise. Figure 9-1 shows a good example of a data visualization that uses a donut chart to show what types of mobile devices people are using. (You can find this image at `www.designyourway.net/blog/inspiration/when-infographics-go-bad-or-how-not-to-design-data-visualization/`.) The 3-D effect makes it very difficult to understand the data.

Figure 9-1: Confusing donut chart displaying usage of most popular mobile devices.

It's also important to ensure that the purpose of the visual is super-clear so that the user has no room for misinterpretation. As we mention in Chapter 5, good data visualizations tell a story at a glance, leaving the reader wanting more. If the data visualization is confusing or misinterpreted, most users get turned off and abandon it. Figure 9-2 (which you can find at the same URL as Figure 9-1) shows an example of a confusing visualization that depicts the usage of social networks. Unfortunately the colors and percentages seem to have no correlation and are therefore very confusing. Can you tell what the visualization is portraying?

facebook — 100%

twitter — 80%

You Tube — 55%

Linked in — 26%

myspace — 10%

Figure 9-2: This confusing infographic shows the usage of top social networks.

To have a little more fun viewing bad data visualizations, visit one of my favorite sites at http://wtfviz.net.

Visual fits the data

The visual has to fit the data. (See Chapter 4 for information about choosing effective charts.) Visuals are more than just charts, however, and certain visuals just don't fit certain data. Usually, you can present data in multiple ways. Your job is to find the most effective way to do so.

You should never use a pie chart, for example, to show data with more than five data points or to display any data set with little to no variation in magnitude. Similarly, you should never use a table or scorecard to show a trend over time. Chapter 14 covers the challenge of choosing the right visual and other pitfalls of data visualizations.

Figure 9-3 shows two visualizations that chart the same data. The line chart at the top is the best option for showing the Sales Margin trend in 2014, because it makes it blatantly clear that the company's expenses are soaring way above its profits. The column chart at the bottom doesn't convey that trend as clearly. Column charts are best used to compare items.

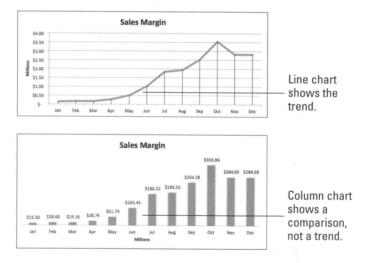

Figure 9-3: The line chart is the better representation of this data.

Exceptions are easy to spot

Whether they're in the form of alerts, comparisons, or outliers, exceptions in the data should be easy to spot in an effective visual. If an exception requires additional deep analysis to understand, chances are that your visual isn't effective.

Exceptions in data visualizations are extremely powerful and can add great value. When users can spot exceptions and decipher them quickly, they know whether immediate, moderate, or light attention is needed. Highlighting exceptions also provides insight into potential trends that may require attention. We discuss this topic in the next section.

Figure 9-4 shows a chart that uses an alert to highlight some of the exceptions in the sales data trend. This image is at `www.metricinsights.com/product/kpi-warehouse/`.

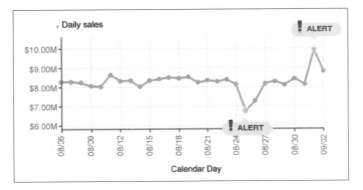

Figure 9-4: This daily sales line chart points out the exceptions using alert colors and a visual cue.

Focus on Insight, Not Hindsight

Sadly, many organizations today look in the rearview mirror when it comes to making critical business decisions. Whether the problems are due to a lack of data availability or the use of the wrong measurements, problems often become visible in the data viz only after they occur. As a result, the user can only react to what has already happened, acting on hindsight.

When you include what we call intelligent data to make your data visualization useful, you try to provide as much insight as possible by using the data to hint at what the future may hold. Using past trends to forecast future behavior is one way to do this. You want to give the user insight so that he or she can be proactive in making decisions that may prevent problems.

The combination of Big Data with a good data visualization can tell you not only where you've been (hindsight) but also where you're going and even how to get there (insight). Therefore, your data visualization should provide a preview of what may be coming next.

Add Visuals to Your Mock-Up

Drum roll! This is the moment you've been waiting for. It's time to add visuals to your storyboard. For the sake of consistency, the examples in this chapter build on the storyboard example from Chapter 7.

This section shows you how to transform your BI storyboard into an effective mock-up. You pull together all the pieces of your storyboard to develop an effective data visualization that your users will adopt and find great value in.

Your BI storyboard has four sections:

- ✔ **Current State:** Where are you now?
- ✔ **Trends:** How did you get here?
- ✔ **Forecast:** Where will you end up?
- ✔ **What-if:** What can you change to achieve or exceed your goals?

At this stage, you should have the main layout of your mock-up completed, with all the required elements (logo, title, and so on) that we discuss in Chapter 8. All the visuals that we discuss in this chapter will be placed into the layout section of the mock up, as shown in Figure 9-5.

Title   Source | Reset | Print | Help | Reports

a.   Section 1 - Current State

Mockup Body

b.   Section 2 - Trends

Mockup Body

Copyright ABC Company

Figure 9-5: The layout section is where 95 percent of the visuals will be housed.

Effective visuals aren't limited to charts, so at times, you may use text or colors in the header and navigation sections to make your message more effective. See Chapter 5 for more details on how to use visual cues to humanize your message and make it more effective.

Before you get into the following sections that describe how to put together our example mock-up, it's important that you understand that the user of the data in the example is Steve Johnson, the senior director of sales for a major toy company, whose main interest is, of course, sales numbers. His division is responsible for more than $2 billion dollars in transactions annually. He's been giving a mandate to grow his business by 5 percent ($100MIL) in the next three years, and he wants to track that goal both on macro (annual) and micro (weekly) levels.

Section 1: Current State

Based on our discussions with our senior sales director and his team, we used our BIDF Blueprint to really understand and document his requirements (see Chapter 8). As a result, in Section 1: Current State, we display two sales-related KPIs to give the user a good view of what is currently happening with respect to the annual and weekly goals. Those two KPIs are

- ✔ **Probability to Hit Sales Target:** Measures the likelihood that the sales reps will hit their sales targets to get their bonuses

- ✔ **Sales:** Measure the actual sales amount on a weekly and year-to-date (YTD) basis

See Chapter 7 for more information about the Section 1: Current State portion of the storyboard.

Using these two measurements, we then do a further evaluation of each to find the most effective way to visualize them on the mock-up, as the following sections illustrate.

Showing the Probability to Hit Sales Target KPI

First, examine Figure 9-6, and note details on this measurement from the Business Intelligence Dashboard Formula (BIDF) Blueprint:

- ✔ **Format:** Percentage
- ✔ **Alerts:** Green if more than 90 percent, yellow if 85 percent to 89 percent, red if less than 84 percent
- ✔ **Viewing Period:** Daily
- ✔ **Reporting Period:** Daily

Execution - Key Metric identification							Monitor	
#	Existing Report	Area	KPI	Chart Views	Format	Viewing Period	Reporting Period	Alerts
1	SalesReport.xls	Sales, Marketing, Finance	Margin	Actual vs. Budget / Forecast	%, $$, numbers, decimals, hrs	Daily	Weekly, Monthly, Quarterly, Annually	1 to -1 = Yellow / 0 = Green / <-1 0r <1 = Red
1	SalesReport.xls	Sales	Probability to hit Sales Target	Show % to date	0%	Daily	Daily	Green if > 90%; yellow if equal to 85% to 89%; Red if <84%
2	SalesReport.xls	Sales	Sales	12 months Trend / Actual		Wkly / YTD	Daily	

Figure 9-6: The BIDF Blueprint with the details of the two metrics for Section 1: Current State.

To further decide how we could most effectively visualize the probability to hit sales target KPI, we closely studied the attributes of it in the BIDF Blueprint, as shown in Figure 9-6, and made a few key observations:

- **Priority:** The Probability to Hit Sales Target KPI should be front and center in the data viz, and easy to read at a glance.

- **Visibility:** The Probability to Hit Sales Target KPI needs to be large enough in size to stand out from the other visuals.

- **Visual:** The appropriate visuals for the Probability to Hit Sales Target KPI are a donut chart to show visual progress and alerts with text to show the actual probability percentage.

- **Color:** The KPI (RAG) red, amber, and green colors must stand out.

- **Interactivity:** The Probability to Hit Sales Target KPI will be updated daily, but it has no drill down so it will not be interactive.

The preceding observations are the exact thought process that our teams go through as we translate the BIDF Blueprint into effective visuals for our mock-up. Please be sure to read through the observations carefully to ensure you understand our logic before moving on. Many data viz fail during the translation process, so this is an area you'll want to spend some time on. The good news is that with experience it becomes much easier to translate your BIDF Blueprint into a mock-up.

After studying the requirements that we gathered and documented from the users in the BIDF Blueprint, we developed the visualization shown in Figure 9-7 using a wireframe tool called Balsamiq. (See Chapter 8 for more details on great wireframing tools.)

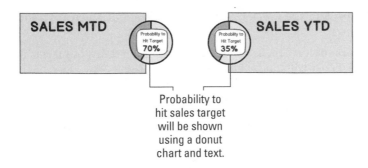

Figure 9-7: Displaying the probability of hitting a target by using two large circles and some text.

In Figure 9-7, notice that the big circles in this visualization were made to stand out from the rectangles. This detail draws attention to the current state and the probability that the goal will be reached.

Showing the Sales KPI

If you look back at the BIDF Blueprint in Figure 9-6, you see that the second KPI is Sales. In the chart view column for this KPI, it says that one of the requested views is actual sales over a 12-month period. To determine the most effective way to display this visual, we need to take a closer look at the other attributes of the Sales KPI:

- **Format:** Dollar ($0,000)
- **Reporting Period:** Daily
- **Viewing Period:** Weekly/YTD
- **Alerts:** None

To further decide how we could most effectively visualize the Sales KPI, we closely studied the attributes of it in the BIDF Blueprint, as shown in Figure 9-6, and made a few key observations:

- **Priority:** The users want to see their actual sales amount to help them gain a sense of their true current state and to relate it to the Probability to Hit Sales Target KPI.

- **Visibility:** The actual sales should be placed next to the Probability to Hit Sales Target KPI.

- **Visual:** The Sales KPI needs some context as discussed in Chapter 5; we can display the actual sales number and a simple horizontal thermometer to let the user quickly identify the progress against the actual sales target for the given time period.

> ✔ **Color:** Red and green colors show if the actual sales are trending up or down.
>
> ✔ **Interactivity:** The Sales KPI will be updated daily, but it has no drill down so it will not be interactive.

When you develop your mock-up, before you place any visuals onscreen, you need to study the BIDF Blueprint and then work to make sense of why and how users would want to see certain data (sales, in this example) represented.

Figure 9-8 shows how the actual sales will be represented on the storyboard.

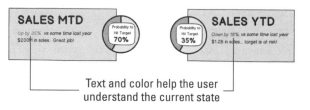

Text and color help the user
understand the current state

Figure 9-8: Add the Sales KPI to the mock-up.

Sometimes it helps to also include a visual. See Figure 9-9 in which we've added a horizontal thermometer to show the actual sales amount versus the target sales amount for the given period. For purposes of this book, we're sticking to the idea of KISS (Keep It Simple, Superstar). Don't be afraid to venture into the visual wilderness and use your creative nature, however.

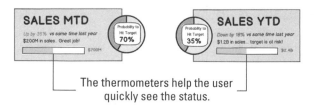

The thermometers help the user
quickly see the status.

Figure 9-9: The Sales KPI is also displayed using a horizontal thermometer to compare the actual against the target.

Section 2: Trends

Section 2: Trends of the storyboard focuses on trends. This section should display how sales got to their current state, whether that state is good or bad. This section explains the history of the KPIs from Section 1: Current State.

In the Trends sections, your visuals should highlight both good and bad stories of Section 1: Current State. For the example of the Sales storyboard we've been using, if a user met or exceeded her sales target, this section displays what she did to get there. For instance, let's say a particular marketing campaign provided a larger than expected ROI (return on investment). That's a factor that directly affects the sales revenue and could explain why the user's probability to hit her sales target may be 110 percent. Trust us: Any sales person would like to know this kind of information.

Similarly, if things aren't going as planned and the user isn't on schedule to meet her sales target, this section shows what's wrong. Section 2: Trends provides great insight to the users and should help to drive proactive behavior.

Techniques for showing trends

There's more than one way to visually represent trends. As always, you should consider the space you have available and the data that you're representing and choose the best possible visual for the job.

For example, you can show upward or downward trends using a simple arrow as shown in this figure. (You can find this image online at www.bu.edu/campaign/2012/08/09/alumni-participation-bu-bucks-the-trends/.)

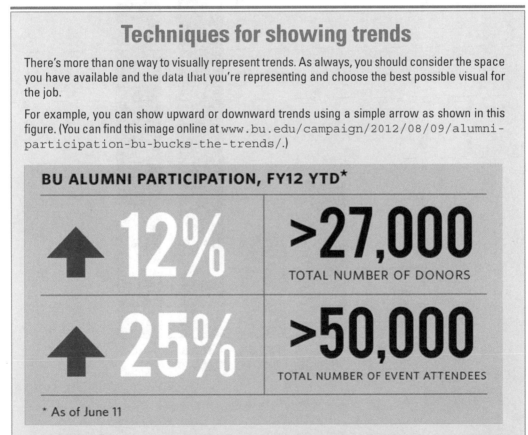

A column chart is also an effective way to show trends, as shown here. (See the original image at http://makanaka.wordpress.com/2012/12/30/global-trends-to-2030-and-the-confusion-of-alternative-worlds/.)

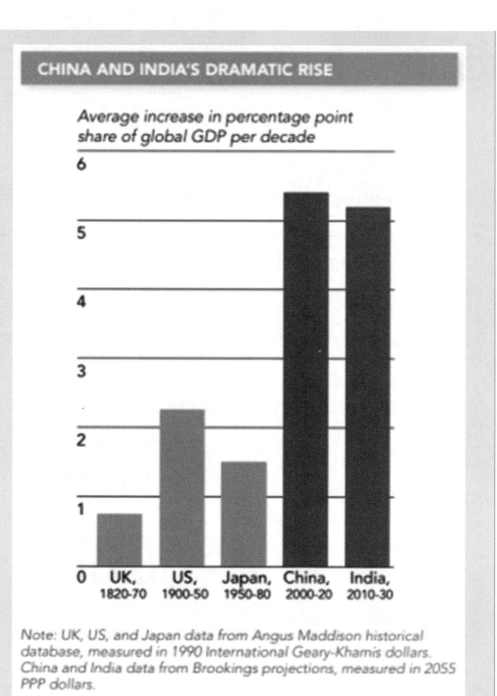

CHINA AND INDIA'S DRAMATIC RISE

Average increase in percentage point share of global GDP per decade

Note: UK, US, and Japan data from Angus Maddison historical database, measured in 1990 International Geary-Khamis dollars. China and India data from Brookings projections, measured in 2055 PPP dollars.

Source: Brookings Institution.

Referring back to Section 1: Current State, it's clear that although our user, Steve Johnson, is on track to meet his MTD (month to date) sales target, his YTD (year to date) is in big trouble, with only a 35 percent chance of meeting the goal. Consequently, we had further discussion and asked, "Can you help us understand what factors would contribute to you exceeding or missing your sales target?"

We then documented those factors in our BIDF Blueprint using the same format that we did for Section 1: Current State. We came up with five measures, but in keeping with our KISS approach, we are using only two for this example:

- **Sales Trend:** Compares the behavior/trend of the sales revenue over a specified period of time.

- **Marketing Campaign Performance:** Displays the performances of the top five and bottom five marketing campaigns and shows their direct effect on the main goal of hitting the sales target.

Many organizations get stuck displaying trends in their data visualizations that have no relation to the bigger picture (the current state). Then they wonder why users don't bother with or trust the data. This lack of information only scratches the surface and forces the user to perform tons of additional analysis to determine the effects of those trends on their goals. You want to avoid this situation. You want your users to get as much of the information they need directly from your visualization.

Focus on showing what we call the *impact* of each visual. For our sales storyboard example, we did this by displaying how the performance of each marketing campaign affected the overall sales. Figure 9-10 shows a way to display impact for the Trends section.

Division	Annual Revenue ▲	Possible Impact
#1 Shirts	$325M	2% I 6.5M
#2 Shorts	$320M	3.2% I 10.2M
#3 Hats	$216M	5.4% I 11.6M
#4 Socks	$100M	6.7% I 6.7M
#5 Skirts	$57M	9.8% I 5.6M

Shows the possible financial impact each product could have on the annual revenue

Figure 9-10: Notice how each marketing campaign affects the sales.

One good thing about trends is they always occur over some period of time, such as hours, days, weeks, months, or even years. Your goal is to show a pattern (if one exists) to explain how the user ended up at his existing current state, as well as to point out any exceptions that may have had a major impact on the current state. You're essentially looking for outliers or patterns in the data that tell a story. Figure 9-11 shows a dual access chart with some outliers circled in red.

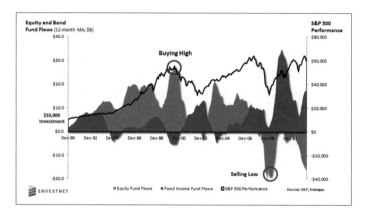

Figure 9-11: The exceptions (highs and lows) are clearly highlighted in this area chart.

Showing 12-month sales trend

If you have another look at the BIDF Blueprint in Figure 9-6, in the Chart View column it specifies that the users want to see a 12-month trend for Sales. As a reminder, the attributes of the sales KPI on the BIDF Blueprint are

- **Format:** Dollar ($0,000)
- **Reporting Period:** Daily
- **Viewing Period:** Weekly
- **Alerts:** None

To determine how to effectively visualize the 12-month sales trend view, we studied all of the attributes of the Sales KPI in the BIDF Blueprint and made a few key observations:

- **Priority:** The users want to see a trend of their sales likely to identify any exceptions or to determine if their sales are trending downward.
- **Visibility:** The 12-month sales view will be shown on a separate chart.
- **Visual:** Line charts are the best representation of trends over time.
- **Color:** Unless the user's sales are trending down, alerts will not be used.
- **Interactivity:** The 12-month trend should have pop-ups for each month to show actual values.

When you develop your mock-up, before you place any visuals onscreen, you need to study the BIDF Blueprint and then work to make sense of why and how users would want to see certain data (sales, in this example) represented.

Figure 9-12 shows a line chart we built using Balsamiq to display 12 months of sales.

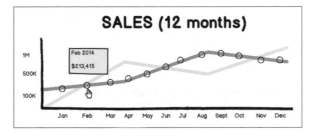

Figure 9-12: The line chart illustrates the trend in sales over a 12-month period.

Showing Marketing Campaign Performance

The second measurement covered in Section 2: Trends is Marketing Campaign Performance. It measures the effectiveness and ROI of each marketing campaign. For instance, if the company invests $200K to run an ad campaign at all the local Target Stores for the holidays and expects a $500K return ($300K gain) but only receives a $450K return, then they received $50K less than expected and their projections need to be adjusted.

Figure 9-13 shows the BIDF Blueprint we've been using after we added a line for Marketing Campaign Performance. You can see what we learned about this metric:

- ✓ **Format:** Dollar ($0,000)
- ✓ **Reporting Period:** Daily
- ✓ **Viewing Period:** Daily
- ✓ **Alerts:** None

Execution - Key Metric identification						Monitor			
#	Existing Report	Area	KPI	Chart Views	Format	Viewing Period	Reporting Period	Alerts	Security
1	SalesReport.xls	Sales, Marketing, Finance	Margin	Actual vs. Budget / Forecast	%, $$, numbers, decimals, hrs	Daily	Weekly, Monthly, Quarterly, Annually	1 to -1 = Yellow / 0 = Green / <-1 0r <1 = Red	HR Only
1	SalesReport.xls	Sales	Probability to hit Sales Target	Show % to date	0%	Daily	Daily	Green if > 90%; yellow if equal to 85% to 89%; Red if <84%	
2	SalesReport.xls	Sales	Sales	12 months Trend / Actual		Wkly / YTD	Daily		
	SalesReport.xls	Marketing Fin	Marketing Campaigns		$0.00	Daily	Daily	NA	

Figure 9-13: Attributes of the Marketing Campaign Performance measurement in the BIDF Blueprint.

To further decide how we could most effectively visualize the Marketing Campaign Performance KPI as a part of the Section 2: Trends view to ensure it fits into the story we want to tell, we again closely studied the attributes of it in the BIDF Blueprint as shown in Figure 9-13 and made a few key observations:

- ✔ **Priority:** After the users are finished with viewing their current state, this is the second layer to explain how they got to the current state.

- ✔ **Visibility:** When marketing campaigns fail or succeed, they directly affect the sales revenue projections and actuals. Hence, Marketing Campaign Performance KPI should be placed either to the right (as users read in a backward Z pattern as we discussed in Chapter 6) or on the right of Section 1: Current State.

- ✔ **Visual:** Because marketing campaigns can make or break sales reps when it comes to hitting sales targets, campaigns that have exceeded expectations or that have been performing below expectations in the past 6 months need to be identified. Essentially, the visualization should show the campaigns that had the biggest effect on the current state of the sales measurement. For our example, we will use a combination of text, a trending icon, and a chart. In addition, marketing campaigns that worked last year may not work this year, so the visualization should highlight any major exceptions that occur from year to year.

- ✔ **Color:** Red and green colors will only be used for the trending icon (an arrow) to show if the actual sales are trending up or down.

- ✔ **Interactivity:** The Marketing Campaign Performance KPI will be updated daily, and it has a drill-down so users can see why those campaigns are failing and identify the top 5 or 10 failing campaigns to give a broader view and more details than we can hold on the data viz.

Figure 9-14 shows a snippet of the Balsamiq mock-up version of the visual that we used to display the Marketing Campaign Performance KPI. Notice that we focus not only on the actual performance amounts but also on the variance (difference in actual versus Target). Magnitude of change is very important when it comes to trends.

Actual sales to date is stated as well as the variance compared to the target and to last year.

Figure 9-14: A wireframe version of how the Marketing Campaign Performance KPI may look.

When we prepared the visualization shown in Figure 9-15, we avoided using only a line chart that would show the trend without providing any actual indication of the magnitude of the gap between actual and planned sales. In the data visualization industry, best practices call for using a line chart when showing trends. We've found that using a line chart doesn't always show enough information, however. The line indicates overall behavior. What the user really needs to know is the change over a given period. In addition, drawing attention to the campaigns that overperformed or underperformed and their direct effect on hitting the annual sales goal makes it easy for users to see how they got to their current state, which is why we used the bar chart on the right of Figure 9-14.

Section 3: Forecast

Finally, it's the moment of truth. The users are on a journey, and now they need to know where they'll end up at a given time if they don't change their current course. Section 3 of the BI storyboard shows the forecast (see Figure 9-15).

Forecast line

Figure 9-15: The forecast is represented on the line chart.

Whereas we make the forecast a separate section for purposes of this book, many of our BIDF students actually embed it in Section 1: Current State. We're making it a separate section in this book to explain the forecast before we show you how you can eventually incorporate it into Section 1: Current State. It's a matter of personal preference and available real estate whether you keep the forecast as a separate Section 3: Forecast or incorporate it into Section 1: Current State. We've seen forecasts executed well both ways. Referring to our BI storyboard model, notice that most of the metrics have already been identified or displayed in previous sections. One of the main metrics in Section 1: Current State, Status of Sales Target, is also shown in Section 3: Forecast. Because we've already defined the metrics in Section 1, we just need to add a visual in Section 3 that shows users where they'll end up at their current pace and, most important, the final outcome with regard to the goal. The forecast projects the outcome based on the current state.

In many organizations, the forecast numbers are often confused with the plan numbers. The difference is that planned numbers are usually preset by someone, whereas the forecast numbers are projected based on the current behavior of the metric (such as sales).

Figure 9-16 shows how to display the forecast number as part of Section 1: Current State.

Adding the forecast to Section 1: Current State is not only a smart use of the limited real estate on your data viz but it also aligns well with the idea of providing the reader a way to see where she's heading compared to where she is today.

We've found that when we add text next to the actual sales figures as we did with Section 1: Current State, and we blatantly tell customers that they're not going to hit their goals, we are often requested to soften the tone. Corporations, especially big ones, are very sensitive to the language being used in any type of internal communication, even data visualizations.

Therefore, we caution you to use phrases that may be more encouraging, such as these:

- ✔ "Heads up! It's time to change course to meet your goals." This type of statement is best used when the numbers are heading in an unfavorable direction.

- ✔ "Don't worry — you can still hit your goals with a few minor tweaks to your master plan." This kind of phrase is best used when the numbers are slightly off and there's still time to fix them.

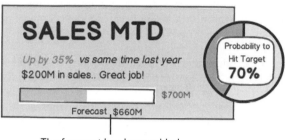

The forecast has been added
to Section 1: Current State.

Figure 9-16: This visualization places the forecast in Section 1: Current State.

These phrases may sound weird for a corporate setting, but you're talking to human beings, not robots. (We cover the practice of using text analysis in more detail in Chapter 5, and we cover the idea of humanizing your visualizations in Chapter 10.) For good examples of humanized data visualizations, visit an infographic-rich site like `http://visual.ly`.

Your goal is to use a visualization to make the user's story personal, relevant, and actionable.

Section 4: What-If

Perhaps the most powerful section, What-If is really the brains of the entire data visualization. Compared with traditional definitions, in the BIDF world, the What-If section provides a series of actionable recommendations, each with a different degree of risk, that users can act on directly to change the course of their future state.

After you've shown the users why their sales have been performing as they have been, you need to show them opportunities to improve their current status. One way to think of the BIDF What-If section is as a bucket of intelligent recommendations that have been generated based on the statuses, trends, and forecasts shown in Sections 1, 2, and 3.

Both data viz developers and stakeholders often avoid the What-If section because of the level of involvement it takes for the business users and analysts to gain the logic that the what-if scenarios are based on and the extensive effort required to develop a database to display the scenarios on the data viz. For this reason, this section isn't used in 95 percent of today's data visualizations. We recommend that after you master the other three sections you work on this area.

Gathering the information for Section 4 usually requires coordinating with data analysts or thoroughly questioning stakeholders to find the root of the problems. Most data viz novices aren't prepared to handle this type of discussion up front, as it takes some practice to engage the stakeholders to complete the BIDF Blueprint (which should be done first). After you master that conversation, it's much easier to steer the What-If discussion with your stakeholders.

We encourage you to get familiar with and think about the What-If section and then build on it as you hone your data viz skills. We could fill a book trying to explain what to cover in Section 4, but we're focusing here on a slightly easier approach that helps you populate it without diving too deep into research conversations with your users. Table 9-2 shows an example of how we could formulate the recommendations based on the information we gathered for our example sales storyboard.

Table 9-2	Section 4 Recommendations	
What-If Buckets	*Options*	*Impact*
Option A Risk level – High Impact – High	Reallocate 100 percent of Campaign A funding to Campaign B.	Increase probability to 98 percent
	Launch a new campaign in the East Coast region based on previous-year sales at a specific store.	Sales increase by $20 million
Option B Risk level – Medium Impact – Medium	Reduce funding of Campaign A to less than 50 percent of the current total.	Increase probability to 75 percent
	Add a discount to an existing promotion to make it more attractive.	Sales increase by $12 million
Option C Risk level – Low Impact – Low to medium	Reduce funding of Campaign A to less than 80 percent of the current total.	Increase probability to 59 percent
	Add an online coupon option to an existing promotion.	Sales by $4 million

If you're new to data viz, we highly recommend that you master Sections 1, 2, and 3 in your first couple of data visualizations before taking on the information in Section 4. Although Section 4 is a game-changer, if you do it incorrectly and the recommendations turn out to be inaccurate or have a negative financial impact, the professional ramifications can be devastating. The recommendations in this section have to be driven and controlled by your business users. Your only aim is to ensure that the data is visualized correctly and that the data (if that's your responsibility) is modeled correctly to produce the most optimal recommendations.

Adding Functionality and Applying Color

· ·

In This Chapter

▶ Humanizing your data viz

▶ Choosing effective colors

▶ Understanding navigation

· ·

*N*ow that you've completed the mockup of each section of your storyboard and added some visuals, it's time to add some functionality and color to your data viz. Adding functionality to your mockup requires that you bring it into your tool of choice. See Chapter 3 for more details on choosing the correct business intelligence (BI) tool to build your data visualization.

This chapter shows you how to develop a mobile-first mentality, add easy-to-use navigation by choosing the correct menu types, and choose and apply an effective color scheme to your data viz.

Adding these formatting and style components is what we refer to as the human side of data viz. Humanizing your data viz is a critical component of any data visualization.

Recognizing the Human Components

As compelling mobile apps continue to evolve, user expectations are at an all-time high. Gone are the days when apps could survive based simply on their usefulness. In the app world, having an attractive and intuitive user interface (UI) is a do-or-die proposition. In the data-viz world, a nice UI has typically been considered to be something that is nice to have, but that school of thought is changing. No matter how great the data is, if your data-viz UI is not user friendly then no one will use it.

Humanizing your visualizations

Adding the human component to your data visualization is a must, though sadly, many people overlook this task.

Following are some easy ways to humanize any data viz:

- ✔ **Use simple navigation.** Imagine having a car with the lock/unlock door buttons hiding under the seat, or a car with the open/close window buttons located in the trunk. Is that a car that you would buy or want to use? Probably not. The same is true of a data viz with confusing menus. It not only frustrates users as they attempt to get to their data but also causes them to stop using it.

- ✔ **Use colors effectively.** When it comes to color, what is effective and ineffective is always subjective. There are always users who don't like a particular color. It's your job to ensure that your data visualization follows some best practices for effectively applying color regardless of the color scheme.

- ✔ **Use intuitive images and visual cues.** One of the most overlooked humanization techniques is to apply easy-to-understand visual cues and images that appeal to the human mind. The emergence of social media sites such as Instagram and Flickr — which have hundreds of millions of users who gather online to share their images — demonstrates that human beings like to see images.

Thinking mobile first

Another thing to consider in the humanization of your data viz is the goal of designing first for mobile users. Let's face it — the use of desktop computers is dwindling. Laptop sizes are shrinking at alarming rates, and mobile phones and tablets are becoming the main choices among users.

With this trend in mind, it's important that you build your data viz first and foremost to fit on mobile devices. If you don't, you risk having very low user adoption.

Here are a few benefits of building mobile visualizations first:

- ✔ **The desktop is included.** If you focus on building your data visualization for a mobile environment, it will certainly be usable on a desktop. Being forced to use a 7-inch screen (the size of most tablets) to display Big Data limits what can and can't be shown in your data viz.

That is why using our Business Intelligence Dashboard Formula (BIDF) method and narrowing down the story to make it concise and useful (see Chapter 7) are so important.

You don't have enough real estate on mobile devices to show everything, hence, you'll be forced to focus on what's needed in the 7-inch display most tablets. Because most desktop screens tend to be bigger than 14 inches, anything that you design for a tablet will likely fit on any desktop as well.

✏ **It forces simplicity.** Another benefit of having limited real estate for your data viz is simplicity. A 7-inch screen can only hold one or two visuals at any given time before scrolling is required. Scrolls or swipes should be limited to two to three to avoid the risk of losing the user. This limit equates to a maximum of six visuals per data viz.

✏ **It encourages easy user access and collaboration.** If you build a house, but it doesn't show up on GPS, visitors will have a problem finding where you live. The same is true of data visualizations. If you don't make your data visualizations accessible on the devices people use most, don't expect to get much foot traffic. Working from home and traveling have become vital parts of most professional careers, so users shouldn't have to sit down and open a heavy laptop to see their data.

✏ **It enhances collaboration.** Giving users a way to take a screen shot and post comments to a collective knowledge base on a topic before making a decision leads to better decisions in less time.

Adding functionality

It's important to understand functionality in the data-viz world: a series of actions that you expect users to take, usually in a sequential manner, that helps them have the most optimal experience with a given data viz. To determine what functionality to choose, ask yourself two questions:

✏ **Where do I want the users to go?** In most cases, when users enter your data viz, you want their eyes to focus on Section 1, their current state. A glance at the current snapshot should let them decide whether they need to address the matter immediately or come back later, based on whether their current state is negative or positive. (Refer to Chapter 7 for a description of the different sections of a storyboard.)

✏ **When the users get where I want them to be in the data viz, what happens next?** The answer to this question is critical, as it dictates what you expect to happen after the users look at the data viz. The users' next steps need to be clear.

Table 10-1 shows several common actions that users may take after they enter a data viz.

Table 10-1	List of Common User Next-Step Actions
Action	**Outcome**
Make a decision	After the user sees the resulting data, he or she decides the next steps, which is your desired outcome.
Use a menu selector	When using menu selectors, the user can filter or drill down into the visualization or even change what's being displayed.
Move to next section	The user understands the message that the data is communicating and needs to move to another section to continue the story.
Share visual(s)	The user decides to take a screen shot and then e-mail all or part of the data viz to someone else for the purpose of gaining collective knowledge or delegating next steps.

Although Table 10-1 doesn't cover every scenario, the list accounts for about 80 percent of the actions a user will take. In this book, we focus on making the actions of using a menu selector or moving to another section intuitive and easy for the user to follow.

To finish defining the functionality, simply ask yourself "What happens next?" until the user makes a decision. Intelligent data helps users make faster decisions.

Choosing navigation by using rules

Imagine having a business that can't be found using one of the popular GPS systems, such as Google Maps. Revenue will suffer, and the business could fail. The same applies to a data viz that has poor navigation. If users can't find their data with little to no effort, they're not coming back. You have to make it crystal clear where you want them to go to see the complete story.

One way to do this is to add navigation to your mock-up. Usually, you add navigation to a data viz through a combination of menus, images, and words.

The good news for data-viz geeks is that the web development industry has tested and set standards and rules for effective ways to include navigation in any user interface.

Take a look at the navigation on two popular websites. The site shown in Figure 10-1 has the navigation across the top and on the left side, and the site shown in Figure 10-2 has the navigation at the top. Both locations are common. Just go to any of your favorite sites, and it's likely that you'll see the same setup.

Top Navigation

Side Navigation

Figure 10-1: Amazon.com uses top/left navigation to guide users.

Top Navigation

Figure 10-2: The CNET website uses top navigation to guide users.

It's also important to note that some data visualizations may not need navigation because they just display data for the purposes of monitoring. A good example of this specific type of data visualization is a dashboard that is used to monitor the number of calls in queue at a call center. The user can take a glance at the data viz on the wall and become aware that he probably needs to wrap up the existing call to be able to address the calls in queue.

The logic behind where to place the navigation on your data viz — be it at the top, left, or bottom rather than in the middle — has to do with the way that most humans read information. Most people tend to read from left to right in a *Z* pattern, as shown in Figure 10-3.

Figure 10-3: The proven reading pattern of most people is in a Z pattern.

Identifying the most popular menu types

You may not realize how heavily dependent you are on menus to navigate your favorite apps and websites. Most people use up to a hundred menus a day without even realizing it! To ensure great navigation on your data viz, you need to choose the right menu type. These include

- ✔ **Menu selectors:** Including such items as drop-down menus, list boxes, radio buttons, and tabs
- ✔ **Navigational icons:** Arrows or text

We discuss each menu type in the following sections.

Menu selectors

A menu selector is a component such as a drop-down menu or list box that enables the user to filter and/or navigate through different data views on a given data visualization.

The most common menu selectors used today include the following:

- **Drop-down menus:** Drop-down menus are among the most popular menu selectors because they're compact and can display a long list of items. At times, however, you shouldn't use a drop-down menu, like when the list of menu options is too long (30 or more), as shown in Figure 10-4.

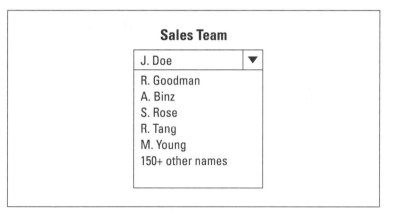

Figure 10-4: The drop-down menu has too many options and is too long.

- **List boxes:** Another very popular option is the list box. Used to display huge lists of data, list boxes are straightforward and work well with huge data sets, as shown in Figure 10-5.

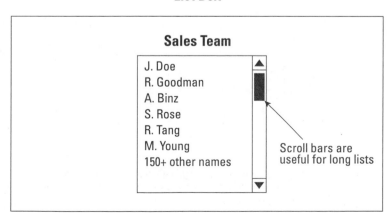

Figure 10-5: A list box with a scroll bar is useful for long lists.

✔ **Radio buttons:** Radio buttons are less popular but work well when you have a small set of selections, as shown in Figure 10-6. We recommend avoiding this menu type if you have more than five options; the display could quickly exhibit data overload.

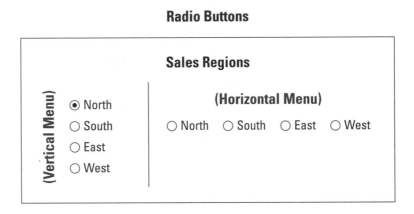

Figure 10-6: Typical radio-button menus.

✔ **Tab sets (vertical or horizontal):** The highest-level menu selector is a tab set. Tab sets are best used when you need to differentiate sections in a collection of visuals. You could use separate tabs to show the visuals for four sales regions (North, South, East, and West) in the same data viz, as shown in Figure 10-7.

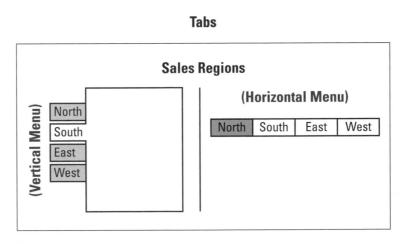

Figure 10-7: Horizontal and vertical tab sets.

Navigational icons

Another way to provide navigation is to use icons, such as arrows or text, to guide the user (see Figure 10-8). These visual cues are easy to read and serve the same purpose as a street sign. They guide the user through the data viz.

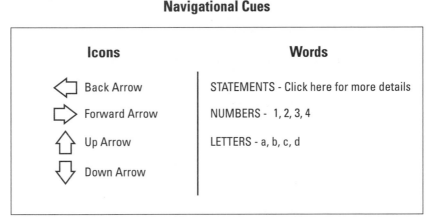

Navigational Cues

Icons	Words
Back Arrow	STATEMENTS - Click here for more details
Forward Arrow	NUMBERS - 1, 2, 3, 4
Up Arrow	LETTERS - a, b, c, d
Down Arrow	

Figure 10-8: Common navigation icons and words used to guide users.

Dipping Into Color

Choosing a color scheme can be one of the most daunting tasks in your data visualization journey. It's the Achilles heel of most newbies. Whether you're working with a user or simply trying to determine what combination to use in your own data viz, the task of choosing effective colors can be difficult.

Many things can go wrong during this phase, including overusing color, using the wrong colors, and using the right colors in all the wrong places.

We've experienced this "color anxiety" firsthand, so we're going to share the best tricks we use to overcome this hurdle. The following guidelines not only eliminate guesswork but also significantly reduce the amount of time you spend choosing the best color for data viz.

Taking advantage of company branding guidelines

One way to determine the right colors is to use the company branding guidelines — a document that many companies develop to ensure that materials produced by the company always look the same. The marketing team usually owns this document, which clearly defines the company's logo, specific colors, fonts, and even shapes or textures that are used on anything that is branded as belonging to the company. If you've never heard of this document, or if you've heard of it but had no idea how it could be of any use to you, you're in for a surprise. In the data-viz world, the company branding guidelines are life-savers, because they take most of the guesswork out of choosing a correct color scheme because you use the colors of the brand.

Two good examples of branding guidelines are shown in Figure 10-9 and Figure 10-10. Figure 10-9 displays a screenshot of the Google Visual Assets page (image found at `www.behance.net/gallery/Google-Visual-Assets-Guidelines-Part-1/9028077`) along with a preview of Google Analytics (image found at `http://upload.wikimedia.org/wikipedia/commons/3/3f/Google_Analytics_Sample_Dashboard.jpg`). Though Google's branding is very simplistic, it does show how Google utilizes its own branding guideline in its analytics displays.

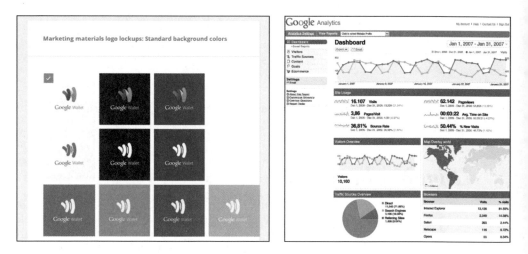

Figure 10-9: Google's Visual Assets Guidelines and its Google Analytics data viz display.

The left side of Figure 10-10 displays the brand standards for Ohio University. The right side of the figure is an infographic on the school's website that utilizes the brand standard very precisely. Also notice the consistency in the website. The quickest way to get a feel for a company's brand, especially in the absence of an available branding guideline, is to take a look at the company's website. You can determine the colors and fonts by taking a peek at the page source code.

Figure 10-10: The screen on the right is an example Ohio University's publicly available branding standards in action.

Why are the branding guidelines such a big deal? You can use the same colors (usually available in pantone or RGB [red, green, blue] format) and use them in your data viz. See Chapter 10 for more on using color in your data visualization.

If you want to check out some examples of branding guidelines, the Logo Design Love website (www.logodesignlove.com/brand-identity-style-guides) lists guidelines for some major organizations, including Walmart and Adobe.

Consider an example section of a sales mock-up. Here are the details we were provided regarding the logo guidelines:

> **Logo colors:** Pantone Cool Gray 10
>
> **Company colors:** Additional colors are red (Pantone 193), brown (Pantone 483), blue (Pantone 280), and green (Pantone 329). (See Figure 10-11.)

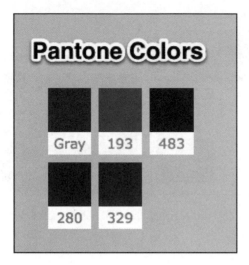

Figure 10-11: A sample color palette.

Figure 10-12 shows some of the colors provided in the company branding guidelines applied to Section 1 of our mock-up. It displays the current state, using two probability circles and a column chart, accompanied by a combination of words and a variety of sizes.

Figure 10-12: Mock-up section uses color from the company branding guidelines.

It's important to note that the use of white space in a data viz enables the user to focus on what is important. Although dark backgrounds may seem to be attractive up front, over time, the user gets tired of trying to view almost-neon text on a dark background. See Chapter 8 for more information.

Choosing colors without guidelines

On the Internet, you can find software to do just about anything — even select your color scheme! In the event that you don't have access to a set of branding guidelines, you can use the following method to create your own color guidelines:

1. Choose a color from the company's logo as a base color.

When you're in doubt, a color like blue is always a safe choice as it's been proven to be among the top sales colors.

2. Go to the Color Scheme Designer website (or some equivalent site).

Color Scheme Designer (`http://colorschemedesigner.com`), which is shown in Figure 10-13, is a free tool that suggests complementary colors.

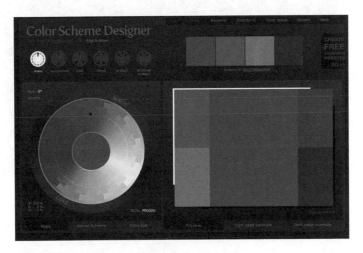

Figure 10-13: Color Scheme Designer.

3. Type in the RGB code for a base color you've chosen.

Figure 10-14 shows where you enter the RGB code.

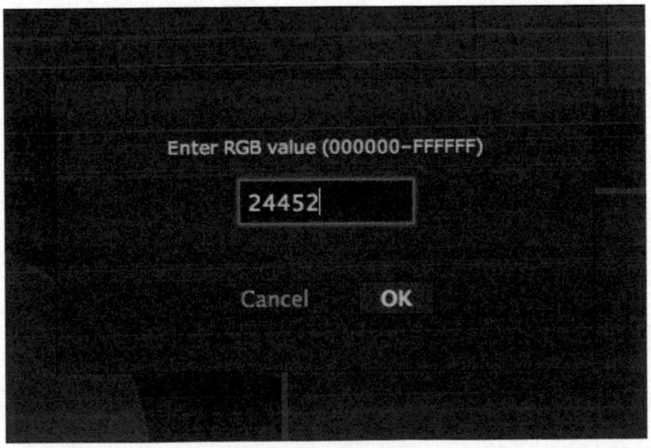

Enter RGB value (000000–FFFFFF)

24452

Cancel   **OK**

Figure 10-14: Enter the RGB value.

4. **Choose the Triad or Tetrad option to get a mixture of colors that goes perfectly with your data viz (see Figure 10-15).**

Triad option   Tetrad option

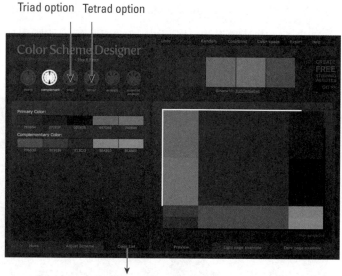

Color List tab

Figure 10-15: Sample color scheme generated by Color Scheme Designer.

5. **Click the Color List tab to see the numbers of the colors in the set.**

After you've finalized your color scheme, you can apply the colors the same way you would if you had company branding guidelines.

Using RAG colors

Some colors in the data-viz color scheme are considered to be sacred, in that they're used only for a specific purpose. These colors are known as *RAG* (red, amber, green) or *alert colors,* similar to the ones you see in traffic stoplights. They hold the same meanings in the data-viz world:

✔ **Red means "Stop!"** Red says that something is going wrong with one of your measurements. If the probability of hitting your sales goal drops below 50 percent, for example, the visual should display red to tell the user at a glance that this measure isn't going as planned and requires immediate attention.

✔ **Yellow means "Proceed with caution."** Yellow means that this measurement needs to be monitored closely. Typically, some action should be taken before the measurement moves to red. Yellow is meant to drive proactive behavior.

✔ **Green means "Everything is okay."** Usually, no action is required when a measurement is green. For this reason, we usually don't show green status in a data viz; that way, the user won't waste mental space.

Figure 10-16 shows how RAG colors are used.

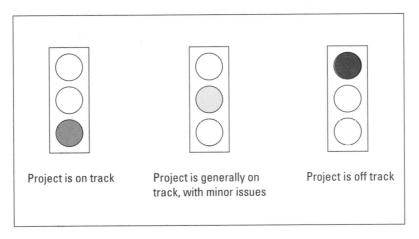

Project is on track   Project is generally on   Project is off track
                       track, with minor issues

Figure 10-16: The meaning of RAG colors in a data viz.

Adding Some Finishing Touches

In This Chapter

▶ Making your links useful
▶ Remembering the legal stuff
▶ Seeing why visual cues matter
▶ Adding location information

*B*efore you can sign off on your data viz as complete, it's time to add a few finishing touches to make it user friendly. This chapter describes how to add useful links such as Print, Share, Help, and FAQ (Frequently Asked Questions).

You also need to include some legal verbiage to ensure that you cover all your bases and protect your artwork. Last, we explain how strategically adding visual cues and some location intelligence can add clarity and curb appeal to your data viz.

As always, the devil is in the details. Although adding a small element such as the Help link may seem trivial, it's critical to the overall adoption and success of your data viz.

Choosing Useful Links

When it comes to determining what links to include, start with actions that you know every user wants to perform, such as Print, Share, and Help. Your goal is to make it as easy as possible for the user to perform these actions.

Where do you place those links on your data viz so that the user can easily find them, but they're not in the way of the critical details you're showing? The website design community has developed specific layout standards that you probably intuitively know, whether you realize it or not.

If you take a closer look at your three favorite websites, you'll notice that all of them have three common areas:

- **Header at the top:** The company logo typically is located here. In some cases, the header includes a navigation bar and some useful links such as the Home, Share, and About links so that the visitor can easily move around the site.

- **Body in the middle:** This area is where the most important data on the page is displayed. It may also house some navigation.

- **Footer at the bottom:** The footer may include copyright labels, a link to a privacy policy, or a link to legal disclaimers, but it may also repeat a set of useful links that help users navigate the site.

Notice that useful links can be included in both the header and the footer of the visualization. Useful links have a clear call to action, and you should place them in easy-to-find locations on the data viz to save the user time and make your data viz easier to use.

Figure 11-1 shows the BIDashboardFormula.com website, outlining the header, body, and footer areas with some of the useful links we discuss in this chapter.

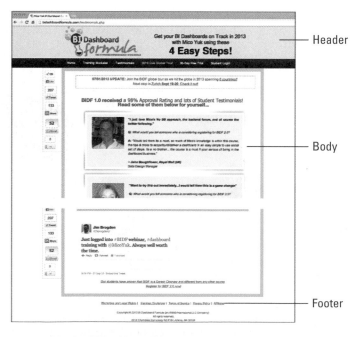

Figure 11-1: The BIDashboardFormula.com website includes the typical header, body, and footer sections.

Introducing six mandatory links

Although you can include many useful links in a data viz, we consider six links to be mandatory:

- ✔ Home
- ✔ Reset
- ✔ Print
- ✔ Share
- ✔ About
- ✔ Frequently asked questions (FAQ)

Some designers argue that these six links are nice to have but not necessary. But most users today expect to do more with less — fewer clicks to get to the home page, fewer clicks to share with friends. Including the six mandatory links makes it possible for users to get where they want to be as quickly as possible.

The following sections describe each of these mandatory links and explain where we recommend that you locate them.

Home

The Home link returns the user to a main page or the first page of your data viz. No matter how simple your data viz is, the user will always need to return home. We recommend that you place this link in the header, as shown in Figure 11-2.

The Home link

| COMPANY LOGO | **DON'S SALES PULSE** | Home | Reset | Print | Store |
| | as of October 07, 2013 | | | | |

Figure 11-2: It's useful to have a Home link on the top of your data viz.

Home links can have different purposes depending on the requirements of your visualization. If you have a one-page data viz, it may be appropriate to have the Home link take the user to the company's intranet site. If the data viz has multiple pages, however, having a Home link to take the user back to page one is highly appropriate. Don't forget to include it!

Reset

The Reset link returns the user to the original state of the data viz before he performed any action on the interactive visualization. When the user clicks the Reset link, the data viz is restored to its original state. This enables the user to start from the beginning of the data viz with the single click of a button.

The Reset button usually sits in the top-right corner of a data viz, as shown in Figure 11-3. This location makes it easy for users to spot. When the links are well designed and properly arranged, the header usually doesn't become too congested with links, buttons, or content.

The Reset link

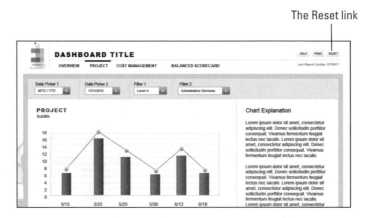

Figure 11-3: A Reset link makes it easy for the user to reset all the settings on the data viz and start from scratch.

Print

The Print function is becoming less popular due to the global push for companies to go green, but it is still a must. Some organizations continue to rely on printed reports; consequently, it's imperative that you make it easy for users to print your visualization.

As shown in Figure 11-4, the Print link usually sits in the top-right corner. It can be represented by a print icon rather than a text link to reduce the amount of real estate it takes up.

The Print link

Figure 11-4: Example of the Print icon on the top right of a data viz.

In some rare cases, you may need to include a more customized Print link. Most Print links default to a portrait shape, whereas most data visualizations require a landscape setting to fit on a standard page.

Be sure to test your Print link. You want to ensure that the user doesn't get stuck figuring out how to configure the data viz in the print preview settings.

Share

The Share link is one of the newest links in the bunch, but it has become one of the most important. Social collaboration has become part of many users' lives. Sharing links increases productivity by allowing users to delegate tasks, gather opinions from other stakeholders, and accelerate the decision-making process. By being able to share and discuss their views on a specific area of the data viz, users can use social collaboration to combine their knowledge and make faster and more informed decisions.

At minimum, you can program a Share link to enable users to share screen shots from their e-mail accounts. When a user clicks a simple link like the one shown in Figure 11-5, a new e-mail message launches automatically. In some cases, the Share link enables the user to send the visualization directly to the company's internal social networking account. In the example shown in Figure 11-5, when the user clicks the link, she will be able to choose among the available social networking options, such as E-mail, Post to Yammer, and Post to Chatter.

The Share link

Figure 11-5: The Share link enables users to connect to some popular internal company social networks, such as Yammer and Chatter.

On most websites, the Share link is in the header (refer to Figure 11-5), although you can also place it in the footer of your data viz. Your primary objective is to make it easy for your users to collaborate.

The Share link doesn't have to be a text link. Another effective and popular method is to use an icon, such as an envelope, or individual social-media icons that indicate which social networks the user can share with. Figure 11-6 shows a site that includes icons for sharing via Facebook, Twitter, and an RSS feed.

Three icons for sharing

Figure 11-6: Share icons on a public-facing Coffee Dashboard data viz.

More information

Although some designers feel that the More Information link is optional, we believe that it's important to include it to provide background or supplemental information. When the user clicks the About link, she sees helpful information such as the purpose of the data viz, who owns it, and any background details that may help her better understand the visualization.

More Information links are often in the headers of websites, and the same holds true for data visualizations, as shown in Figure 11-7. One school of thought is that the About link should be displayed in the footer because it's less important than the links that are placed in the header. That said, it's really up to your preference and the available real estate on the data viz.

THE ULTIMATE TRAVEL CHALLENGE DASHBOARD
Making Informed Decisions in a Fast-Paced Environment

More Information

Figure 11-7: On this data viz, the More Information link is an icon.

If your data viz project has a small audience, you probably can engage all your users during the entire BI Dashboard Formula process. However, when it comes to Big Data and big enterprises, it is virtually impossible to get your entire audience involved. On projects for which you haven't been able to engage all users during the development of your data visualization, a More Information link that provides solid details about the project is important for establishing credibility and also for providing context for what is being displayed.

Frequently asked questions (FAQ)

The FAQ link is also on most websites, and it's critical for every data viz. It's virtually impossible to answer all the questions any user may have, but you make the user's life much easier when you provide answers to the top ten questions on an FAQ page. It can be shown as an icon or a text label, as shown in Figure 11-8.

Information in the FAQ may range from explaining how to complete some tasks with the interactive elements of the visualization to telling users where to find a particular element. You may decide to include contact information in case a user needs additional help.

Ideally, you want to order the questions based on how frequently they're asked. When you first launch your data viz, you may find it challenging to arrange the questions in order of importance. When you're unsure of the order, take an educated guess and then arrange the questions in order of importance based on information you receive during the user testing phase. You can also run the final list by your super-users to request their feedback.

The FAQ link

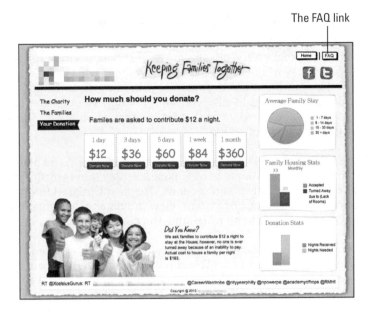

Figure 11-8: The FAQ link.

The FAQ link usually sits neatly next to the About link. As it has a good deal of textual information, it usually works best as a pop-up or mouseover window.

The FAQ link is a great place to include general information, clarification on any important items, or a brief explanation of how to use the data viz. If you want a more visual representation for your FAQ and other help information, or if you are tight on available space, consider using a ? (question mark) link.

Some data viz experts suggest that the need to include an FAQ button is a sign that the data viz is too complex and therefore requires a manual to assist the user. Based on our experience, no matter how clean your data viz is, users always have questions — some of which may seem trivial. The main goal of the FAQ is to help users address those questions as fast as possible so that they can proceed with reviewing the data viz. It's better to make the information readily accessible than to have users who are frustrated because they have questions for which they can't easily find answers.

You should consider the FAQ section to be a living part of the data viz that is subject to change based on the feedback you receive from users after the data viz is launched. In addition, be receptive to requests about the context, definition, or location of any component of your data viz. Some of those requests may turn into refinements of your data viz; others will be information that you can add to the FAQs.

Including a last updated timestamp

With the rise of Big Data, users need to have real-time information available because they depend on the latest and greatest data to drive proactive decision-making. Working from old data — which is what most organizations are still doing — undermines the value of your data viz and usually leads to reactive decision-making. Ideally, you want the data to update every time a user logs in to review the data so that he can make timely decisions about the appropriate course of action.

You can easily let users know the last time the data was refreshed by including that information as simple text. You can display it in terms of month, day, and year or hours, minutes, and seconds. The Last Updated information is particularly useful for your users who view the data on a regular basis. It provides an idea of how fresh or reliable the current data is.

The most popular location for this information is at the right end of the footer, as shown in Figure 11-9. (You could include it in the header instead, if you prefer.) Typically it is displayed using a small font. You want to make the information available if the user is looking for it, but you do not want it to distract from the more important components of the visualization.

The Last Updated
information

Figure 11-9: The last updated timestamp is usually in the footer.

Many organizations pull data from multiple sources, and it's often difficult to have all the data updated at the same time. If your data viz is built from multiple sources, you can provide Last Updated information in two ways:

- **Display the oldest date:** By providing the last updated date of the system with the oldest data, the user gets an idea of how old the most out-of-date piece of information is. This solution is generic, but it's a good start to addressing the issues created when you're using multiple data sources.

- **Display individually updated dates and times:** Although it may prove to be complex and may add clutter if you execute it incorrectly, an alternative solution is to display the last updated date and time for each section or measure of your data viz.

You want to include the most up-to-date and frequently refreshed information at the forefront of your data viz, with less-frequently updated details at the side or bottom of your data viz.

Adding Legal Stuff

Like any good piece of art or specialized system, your data viz is a valuable piece of your company's intellectual property. Therefore, it's critical that you include some information to protect the user and the distribution of the data viz.

Two important pieces of information that you may want to include to protect your company are the copyright and the terms and conditions.

Embracing the copyright

Some people believe that including a copyright on a data viz is optional because it consumes too much space. We recommend that you always add one, however.

Any data viz that you produce automatically becomes the property of your company. In the age of social collaboration and sharing, it's easy for a screen shot of a data viz to float outside company walls. For this reason, you must ensure that anyone outside the company who views this data viz is aware of the following facts:

✔ The data viz is the legal property of your company.

✔ The data viz should not be used without permission from your company unless otherwise stated.

The footer is the most appropriate place for copyright information (see Figure 11-10); that's the location where many websites place it. Like the Last Updated text, the copyright text should be big enough that it's legible but small enough that it doesn't draw attention away from the data viz itself.

#5	Buitoni	>	↓ $231K	59%		#5	Non-DSD	>	↓$1.4B	

Select One for
More Details

Copyright © 2013 Nestle, Inc.   Last Report Date: 03/12/13 12:01pm

The copyright
information

Figure 11-10: The copyright information is often placed in the footer.

Mico has seen individuals illegally use screen shots of data visualizations in presentations. In one severe case, this led to a lawsuit. Millions of dollars in damages were awarded to the company who owned the copyright of the data viz that was illegally used. It's better to be safe than sorry, which is why we advise you to include a copyright on all your data visualizations.

Delving into terms and conditions

Another useful link that you may want to include in your data viz is Terms and Conditions. The terms and conditions spell out how and when the data viz may be used outside its intended use.

Similar to any content-rich piece of work, such as a company's profit and loss statement or the marketing ROI (return on investment) sheet, a data visualization often contains sensitive information that should not be viewed outside the company. By defining who may review and use the visualization in the terms and conditions, you legally define what is acceptable from a use standpoint. Explicitly stating the guidelines makes anyone who goes against the defined terms of use liable for legal damages.

To avoid attracting the user's attention unnecessarily, you should format the Terms and Conditions link in a small font so that it doesn't draw attention away from the important content of the data viz. Preferably you should place it in the footer, as shown in Figure 11-11. To keep things simple, we recommend linking to your company's Terms and Conditions text on the company website.

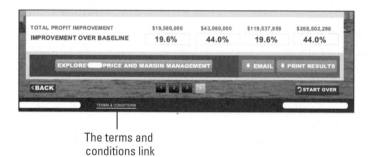

The terms and
conditions link

Figure 11-11: Terms and Conditions link.

Although including these links to legal information may seem to be a bit out of scope, you'd be surprised by how easily data visualizations can be misused. The safest approach is to contact your company's legal department and get specific wording for the terms and conditions information. Be proactive.

Discovering Visual Cues

Have you ever taken a long road trip? You probably remember seeing road signs warning you of upcoming construction zones, accidents, or other unexpected roadblocks that required you to modify your original plans. We're sure that you were grateful to see signs like "Construction 5 miles ahead on left," which provided you enough notice to decide to proceed forward and risk being delayed or to find an alternative route. Those types of road signs are *calls to action.* They enable you to decide which route to take so you can avoid being stuck in a construction-zone traffic jam.

Like road signs, visual cues in data visualizations are helpful to users. *Visual cues* are combinations of text and shapes that are strategically placed to draw attention to a specific area or enforce a call to action.

Figure 11-12 shows an example of some popular visual cues that may be used to draw the user's attention to various exceptions or calls to action in a data viz.

The icon
provides a visual
alert to a problem

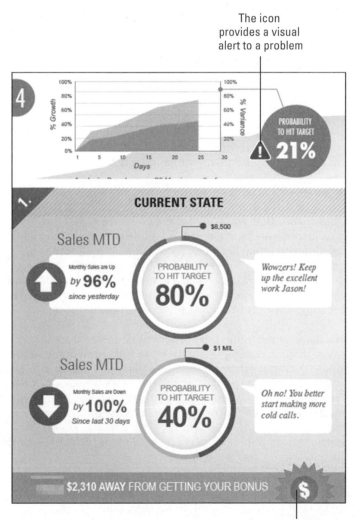

The dollar
sign cue emphasizes
the bonus

Figure 11-12: Visual cues add clarity to the message.

The most effective visual cues are dynamic and appear only when needed. As shown in Figure 11-12, effective visual cues are often a good combination of colors and shapes. They can be graphical icons or only text. The one common theme is that they stand out at a glance.

One common method of providing visual cues is through conditional formatting or alerts. Colors can imply what the current situation is. Red, for example, automatically implies some type of problem or risk associated with a given area or measurement. Green, on the other hand, implies that all is well and no further action is required. See Chapter 10 for more information about using color in your visualizations.

Adding Location Intelligence

Geographic apps, such as Google Maps, help people find their way around unfamiliar locations via mobile devices. One particularly useful app called Waze uses social collaboration, in which drivers inform one another of current road conditions. These types of navigation apps have given rise to the concept of *location intelligence,* which is the mashup of information that can be used to provide enriched data for navigating the world.

Although the specific use cases for including location intelligence in your data viz are broad, it's important not to get distracted by the alluring nature of maps and ensure that you truly have a good use case first. This chapter takes a look at a few areas where maps can be used to help organizations gain critical insights and make better decisions.

Figure 11-13 shows how you can use a combination of branding and visual cues to make your data viz compelling. This coffee data viz displays some very interesting stats about the world's coffee consumption.

Traditional data visualization best practices consider maps to be an inefficient way to display data because they use too much real estate on an already-limited screen. Although we agree that some maps don't make efficient use of space, we feel that as the use of mobile devices with built-in location tracking evolves, there are good uses for maps in the world of data viz. Some effective use cases for maps include the following:

- **Transportation:** Data involving any kind of motor vehicle or fleet is a great scenario for using maps.
- **Retail:** Indoor mapping is a hot topic that continues to gain steam as technology evolves. Putting intelligence around foot traffic in a retail store can tell a company a lot about their consumers.

Google Maps
being used directly
in a data viz as
a heat map

Figure 11-13: This data visualization uses Google Maps as a heat map
to show which states drink the most coffee.

- ✔ **Financial:** Looking at financial data geographically is a great way to identify areas for improvement or trends in specific regions.

- ✔ **Marketing:** Demographic information in the marketing world has determined where and when advertisers choose to place their valuable ads. With the rise of built-in location technology, it's easier than ever for advertisers to target the correct markets for their ads.

Compared with traditional charts and graphs, maps are a lot easier for users to digest. Their interactive nature helps users who are already accustomed to touching a screen to make changes. The widespread popularity of Google has made using maps a familiar and comfortable experience for many users.

We consider incorporating location intelligence to be a luxury in the data visualization world right now, although in the near future, it may become the norm as mobile use continues to grow and Big Data continues to call for more innovative ways for data to be presented.

12

Exploring User Adoption

In This Chapter

▶ Encouraging user adoption

▶ Measuring user adoption

▶ Marketing to increase adoption rates

*E*verything you've done up to this point has been preparation to meet your most important goal: getting a high user adoption rate for your data visualization. Although this may seem obvious, user adoption (UA) is an afterthought in many organizations. It's the thing that everyone focuses on *after* the solution is rolled out to users.

Big companies in particular invest millions of dollars in business intelligence (BI) solutions, which includes developing and deploying data visualizations. But they drop the ball when trying to facilitate high UA rates. They squander both their limited budget and the opportunity to ensure that users get insights from the data.

According to a study done by Cindi Howson, a well-known BI analyst, author, and founder of BIScorecard (http://biscorecard.com), the average UA rate for data visualizations is between 25 and 35 percent. Contributing factors to the low adoption rates were tool complexity (existing tools are too hard for users to use), lack of agility (existing systems make it difficult to adjust to ever-changing business needs), and lack of collaboration during the process. You can read more about the barriers to user adoption at www.indicee.com/blog/breaking-down-barriers-to-bi-adoption-or-anyone-for-another-round-of-pin-the-report-on-the-it-guy/.

In addition, a BI report posted by Gartner in February 2012 estimates that 70 percent of global business intelligence projects undertaken between 2012 and 2014 will fail. Those odds aren't very encouraging if your project includes data visualizations.

This chapter explains what UA is and how to avoid UA traps. It also provides suggestions of things that will help increase your user adoption rate.

Understanding User Adoption

User adoption (UA) is defined as the measure of how much of the intended audience uses the provided solution (in this case, the data visualization). This concept gets a bit murky, however, when you delve into what should actually be measured. Should you measure how many times the data viz is being viewed or the average length of time for which the data is viewed? Perhaps you should measure how many times the data is used to conduct exploratory activities.

The secret of measuring UA is that UA is a combination of many elements. In the business data world, UA isn't just a measure of use but also a measure of the value added to a user.

Considering Five UA Measurements

As you begin to analyze UA rates, you need to understand the following five metrics:

- **Frequency of use:** Frequency of use measures the number of times an individual user uses your data viz. To gain an accurate number, you want to make this metric an average based on overall frequency of use.

- **Interval of frequency of use:** This measures when your data viz is actually being used, as in time of day, month, quarter, year, and so on. For example, you could look at data that has been used between January 2013 and December 2013. Interval of frequency of use involves how often the data being displayed is updated, but it should measure when users access the data viz and perhaps when they find the most value.

- **Area of frequency of use:** This metric is one of the most important to consider. It tells you which sections of the data viz users visit most. It also tells you what areas need to be enhanced or removed from future updates. Finally, it provides a clear focus on what is most valuable to the user. When you see what is used and what is ignored, you get a clear idea about what is truly useful to viewers.

✔ **Type of use:** Measuring how a data viz is actually being used may be a bit tricky, but it's critical to the long-term adoption and success of the tool. If you build a data viz that has drill-down capability, and no one ever clicks to go to more details, that particular feature (or type of use) isn't providing much value to the user.

Unfortunately, many of the data viz tools or systems in the market lack the ability to track UA metrics. We recommend doing monthly or quarterly polls or surveys of your users to gain insight into how, when, and for what purpose the data viz is being used. Doing your own investigation is the only sure-fire way to ensure that you can provide continuous improvements to your data viz so that it will be continually used by your audience.

If you find that users are frequently exporting the raw data in a visualization, that's a clear indication that users don't trust the data viz itself and are using the data viz as nothing more than an export tool. This measure in conjunction with the frequency of use metric tells you a lot about the actual value, or lack thereof, that the users are getting from the data viz.

✔ **Number of total users compared with targeted audience size:** This metric is perhaps the most popular measure of user adoption and is best measured as a percentage. You derive it by taking the total count of the intended audience and the number of users who are actually using the data viz and expressing that figure as a percentage. Suppose that you build a data viz for a sales organization of 500 people. If 50 of those people access the data viz on a regular basis, you have a 10 percent UA rate.

Marketing to Data Viz Users

If you think that when you're done building your data viz that you can simply send an e-mail with the subject "The Sales Pulse app is now available" and users will come flocking, you're going to be very disappointed. This scenario almost never happens. In fact, you can count on users meeting your e-mail with great indifference.

One study found that most applications or solutions that are built for business users have low adoption rates simply because the users were never aware of the application to begin with. You have to put some effort into making your audience aware of your product and the ways that users can benefit from it.

To combat low UA rates, the first thing you need to do is put on your marketing hat. Just like marketing e-mails and thousands of ads that users are exposed to on a daily basis, users will see your data viz as just another app.

It won't stand out unless you do something to market it. To gain the attention of your audience, you need to provide a reason for them to use your data viz and then provide reasons for them to return to it repeatedly.

We have some foolproof ways to boost UA. Many of the suggestions are part of our BI Dashboard Formula (BIDF) program. The following sections list some of the most important techniques for marketing to your users.

Ensure data availability and accuracy

This technique is of key importance. If users can't trust your data, your data viz will never be used. Period. Ensure that your data viz is always painting accurate pictures of the correct data. If the data is found to be unavailable or unreliable for any reason, users are unlikely to revisit the data viz.

To help users believe that your data is reliable, you can look at the data from two different perspectives. They are:

- **Internal company data:** Typically when you use internal data you want to work hand in hand with your IT department to select the most current, error-free data. They will know what holes exist in the data they have. Establish a good working relationship with them so that they will freely tell you the good and bad about the data. If you point fingers or try to blame them for what's missing, you will ensure failure. You also want to make sure that they have been told that your project is a high priority or they may relegate your requests to the end of a long queue.

- **External data from government agencies and other public or private sources:** If you are using this type of data, make sure to provide the source notes. Some users may want to look at the raw data themselves just to be sure it's trustworthy. Others will take your word for it, but if you have no references, you run the risk of appearing unserious, and the data viz will be discarded.

Use buy-in and ownership to engage users

You want to ensure that you're targeting the correct key performance indicators (KPIs) and gaining the audience's buy-in. This is also critical from future advertising and word-of-mouth standpoints. Users will tell others about the value of your data viz, which will help others find and use it.

Give each data viz the right name

We can't emphasize enough how important a name is. This is certainly true of book titles and movies. Also, think about how many e-mails and Twitter hash tags go viral because of their titles.

Great data visualizations use words that directly describe what they show. Consider the fact that many people around the world have been told by their doctors to cut down on their salt intake. Figure 12-1 shows a visualization called Salt Mountains, in which salt intake is represented by peaks of various heights. The catchy title goes a long way toward grabbing the interest of readers. You can see the original image at `www.nextgenerationfood.com/news/salt-levels-in-our-food`.

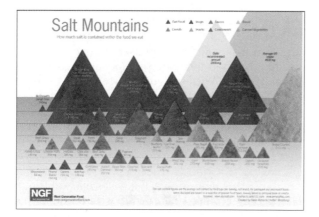

Figure 12-1: Visualizing the salt found in the foods we eat.

Use internal social media platforms and intranets

Many organizations have internal social media platforms, such as Salesforce Chatter and Yammer (`https://www.yammer.com`), which is like a corporate version of Facebook for enterprises.

As soon as a data-viz project launches, create an internal company group by using a tool such as Yammer and invite your team to join the community. It's a great way to create excitement by

- ✔ Posting regular visual updates
- ✔ Adding new screen shots
- ✔ Starting conversations about a particular data viz
- ✔ Highlighting the comments of expert users

Using a social network to discuss upcoming meetings or interesting trends in the data is a great way to attract other users and provide a place for the data viz to grow and attract new users.

Go live on internal platforms

You should treat the announcement of your data viz as you would treat the marketing for a product launch. Depending on the size of your audience, the cost of the data viz, and effort required, you may be able to go live on a social media platform. Your announcement can be as simple as conducting a short webinar for users or as big as a formal event with keynote speakers, prizes, and live use cases presented by your superusers (the major stakeholders).

Do away with training

When someone says that he's going to train users to use his data viz, that statement is a sure sign that he's living in the Dinosaur Age. Ease of use (EOU) is in, and training is out! With the emergence of apps that take two seconds to download and another three seconds to start using, few people will tolerate the need for training. That's why keeping things simple is so important. Apps are successful because they do one thing, and they do it very well. Follow the same line of thinking for your data viz, and it will prove to be successful.

Make sure that the data viz looks great

A house that's for sale needs to have curb appeal; it has to look good from the street so that buyers will want to check out the inside. In the same way, your data viz needs to look good so that people will want to dive deeper into it. Without providing an attractive package, you won't be able to get users to enter the data viz, so why would you expect them to use it? Having a good user interface is a must.

Provide 24/7 accessibility

Allowing users to access your data viz anytime and anywhere is critical for user adoption. With the click or tap of a button, they should be able to view and use your data viz regardless of what device they're using: a mobile device, a tablet, a company laptop, or a desktop computer.

Provide speed and reliability

Yes, speed is a huge factor! Just imagine accessing an app on your phone and then having to wait a long time for it to load, but it crashes after 10 seconds. Most users instantly delete an app that performs that way, and a smaller percentage of users will take the extra step of providing bad feedback in a review. The same goes for your data viz. If your data viz doesn't work correctly and quickly, you can expect users to give up on using it — or, worse, to spread the word to other users that the data viz is a dud.

A Gartner report released about 7 years ago stated that the average user has a 5- to 8-second attention span, after which he or she simply switches to something else. Based on our experience, we would even suggest that the evolution of smartphones has reduced the average user attention span to as low as 2 seconds. This means that if you're unable to load data within that time frame, you'll lose most of your users. If the data viz crashes, it's likely that the users are never going to return and that they'll lose confidence in the application and in you.

Speed the delivery of your data viz

Delivering your data viz in a short cycle is a key component of building and maintaining momentum with your user base. You can use this momentum to build interest for future releases. We recommend that you deliver even the most complex data viz in two to three months maximum and tag it as a *proof of concept*. This usually sets the stage for great future releases and opens discussions about how to further enhance the application.

Taking six months to a year to build and release your first data viz is a surefire way to ensure that you'll have no users.

Part IV

Putting Data Viz Techniques into Practice

COMPANY LOGO

DON'S SALES PULSE
as of October 07, 2013

MENU1 | MENU2 | MENU3 | MENU4 | MENU5

a. TITLE SECTION GOES **HERE**

SALES MTD
Up by 5% *vs. same time last year*
$100M yet to go to achieve target!

120K | $500M
Target

PROBABILITY TO HIT TARGET
50%

PROBABILITY TO HIT TARGET
50%

SALES YTD
Down 5% *vs. same time last year*
$5.6B yet to go to achieve your target!"

2.5B | $5B
Target

b. TITLE SECTION GOES **HERE** ● FILTER OPTION ● MTD ○ YTD

# LAB1	⊕ LABEL2		☕ LABEL3	⌁ LABEL4		# LAB1	♯ LABEL2		∿ LABEL3	⚖ LABEL4	
#1	Option 1	❯	⬇ $100M	10%		#1	Option 1	❯	⬆ $5.0B	1.4B	2B
#2	Option 2	❯	⬇ $100K	10%	THE BOTTOM **5**	#2	Option 2	❯	⬆ $5.0B	1.4B	2B
#3	Option 3	❯	⬇ $100K	10%		#3	Option 3	❯	⬆ $5.0B	1.4B	2B
#4	Option 4	❯	⬇ $100K	10%	👎	#4	Option 4	❯	⬆ $5.0B	1.4B	2B
#5	Option 5	❯	⬇ $100K	10%	ℹ Select One for More Details	#5	Option 5	❯	⬆ $5.0B	1.4B	2B

Copyright © 2013 Your company.

Last Report Date: 03/12/13 12:01pm

In this part . . .

✔ Look at evaluations of real data visualizations from the comfort of your arm chair to see what others have done wrong and how their work can be made better.

✔ See how to increase user adoption of your all your data viz creations.

✔ Get the information you need to avoid the pitfalls most new users face.

Evaluating Real Data Visualizations

In This Chapter

▶ Using a data viz worksheet

▶ Analyzing examples of data visualizations

*I*t's easy to look at data visualizations in a superficial way and just enjoy the effect of the visuals. Some visualizations are dazzlingly interactive; others are funny or clever. But when it comes to real-world business data, the stakes are high.

The true power of a data visualization is realized when it provides insight, tells a story, and sheds light on key issues. These insights would be overlooked if they were presented in other, less visual formats.

In this chapter, we provide a worksheet that you can use to evaluate data visualizations, whether you created them or someone else did. We also show you some real examples of data visualizations so that you can see what works and what doesn't. Feel free to try out the worksheet as you examine the examples!

Analyzing Data Visualizations by Category

There's no better way to build confidence in your own data viz choices than to know how to evaluate what you're looking at. A worksheet that guides you through the major data viz categories is a must.

We've compiled the categories into Table 13-1, which you can use as a worksheet as you're evaluating data visualizations that you use or create. The categories we've included in the worksheet are described in detail later in this chapter. As you evaluate data visualizations, make notes about your impressions of how the data viz succeeds (or falls short) in each of the categories.

The following sections describe the categories in detail.

Table 13-1	Data Visualization Categories	
Category	*Items to Consider*	*Notes*
Big-picture considerations	Simplicity	
	Data overload	
	Chart choice	
	Metadata	
Color	Choice	
	Consistency	
Design issues	White space	
	Layout	
	Table use	
	Icons	
	Duplication	
	Clear sections	
	Personalization	
Text formatting	Size	
	Labels	
	Consistency	
	Cut-off text	
Menus	Choices and placement	
	Filtering	
	Location of filters	
Interactivity	What if	
	Location intelligence	
Design for mobile	Text	
	Images	

Big-picture considerations

The *big-picture considerations* are the general ones that you make about design, quantity of data, and format when you're beginning to create your data viz. These considerations include

- **Simplicity:** Simplicity is key to making your data viz usable. You want to eliminate everything that isn't essential. Don't use a feature just because it looks pretty. Everything in your data viz must have a function.

- **Data overload:** Bombarding your user with too much data is as bad as not giving the user enough data. Test your visualizations with a small focus group to see whether users are overwhelmed by the quantity of data. If they are, you know that you need to make changes before releasing the data viz to your full audience.

- **Chart choice:** The type of chart you use is important. It can be helpful to try several types of charts before you decide which one is best. When you place your specific data into a chart type, you can check to see whether the visual representation enhances or obscures the story the data is telling.

- **Metadata:** *Metadata* is information about the source of your data. It tells you when you obtained the data, for example, or where you got it. Metadata helps you give context to your user. Without context, the user has to make up his own interpretation of the data viz, which wastes time and could be incorrect.

Color

Color has a major impact on your data viz, so you want to choose wisely. In "Evaluating Data Visualizations," later in this chapter, we present several data visualizations that demonstrate poor color choices. You'll see that the colors used instantly deflate the value of the data viz.

Whatever colors you choose, you have to be consistent in how you apply them. You're probably familiar with the idea of color coding, in which a particular color stands for one concept. You can have blue signify sales data, for example. Every time you use blue, the users know that they're looking at data about sales. If you're consistent in how you apply color, you help your users understand data at a glance.

Design issues

Understanding some key design issues makes creating a data viz easier:

- **White space:** One important component of any good design is white space. In the various visualizations that we show later in this chapter, you see that effective use of white space helps separate a good data viz from a bad one.

- **Layout:** You must decide how the features of your data viz will be laid out before you start positioning data. Check out an example of a good layout in data visualization 6, later in this chapter.

- **Tables:** Think carefully about using tables in a data viz, and use them in small doses. Using a big table defeats the purpose of using visuals.

- **Icons:** Icons are great communicators, but don't get carried away with stylish ones that add no real meaning.

- **Duplication:** Duplicating data is a waste of important real estate. Err on the side of simplicity.

- **Discrete sections:** Make sure that data items don't overlap so that data won't be misinterpreted.

- **Personalization:** As you see in data visualization 8, later in this chapter, the use of a personal photo enhances the entire visualization as well as provides useful information.

We cover each of the following topics in more detail in Chapter 6.

Text formatting

Text plays a critical role in giving your data viz the context users need to quickly understand what's being displayed. When you add text, pay attention to the following aspects:

- **Size:** If text is too small or too large, it interferes with users' understanding of the data viz. Don't make people squint!

- **Labels:** Clear labels make a huge difference, but data viz designers often forget to include them because they think that everyone in the audience knows what's being shown. Your users shouldn't have to solve a mystery to get to the true meaning of your data viz. Use explicit labels.

- **Consistency:** Using too many font styles, colors, and sizes can make your data viz look like a ransom note. Limit yourself to two fonts, and be consistent in their use.

- **Cut-off text:** Text that runs off the edge of the data viz or that's covered by a graphic is a serious blunder. Don't make your users guess what the text says. They may guess incorrectly, and that outcome could be as bad as the outcome of providing incorrect data.

Menus

Most users spend a lot of time online; consequently, they have certain expectations about how menus work. Your users rely on the menus in your data viz to navigate the data you're providing, so the way you use the menus is important. You need to take the following aspects of your data viz into consideration:

- **Location of menu options:** Intuitively, you know that the locations of menu options are critical to their use. Look at other data visualizations to see how other designers implement menus.

- **Filtering:** Filtering removes nonessential data. It sets parameters like date range or data type. You want to prevent your users from having to sift through one big data dump. It's just as important to determine what data goes out as it is to determine what goes in.

Interactivity

When you make it possible for users to use interactive features to drill down and get exactly what they need from a data viz, you ensure that they'll return to the visualization on a regular basis. It's essential to figure out how a data viz will be used before you create any interactive features. The following list describes some types of interactivity you can consider:

- **Develop what-if scenarios.** Talk to major stakeholders about the scenarios that they believe are most important. What-if simulations can produce great insights into how users will work with the visualization.

- **Implement location intelligence.** Location intelligence is the capability of the data viz to sort data according to location (see Chapter 11). When you mash up data with its location, you can pull out insights that you wouldn't see if you weren't combing location data with your primary data. You would have no way to determine that sales were very high in a small region in the Northwest, for example, unless you could parse that data. You certainly couldn't guess at what the location was without identifying it.

Design for mobile

As we discuss in Chapter 6, mobile layouts are no longer optional. You need to test your data visualizations to make sure that they're readable on tablets, smartphones, and other portable devices.

Responsive design refers to a layout's capability to modify according to the device on which it's being viewed. It's key to have grids that can be reformed for each device. Visual presentations on the web and mobile devices rely on a standard way of placing items called a *grid*. If the grid resizes itself properly on each device, the design remains intact.

In addition, images must be flexible so that none of the data is cut off. This means that if an image is able to make itself proportionately smaller or larger to fit the screen, you don't lose any part of the image.

Evaluating Data Visualizations

In this section, we provide ten visualizations and describe what's good and bad about each of them. Keep Table 13-1 handy so that you can see how we evaluate each category.

Data visualization 1

Figure 13-1 shows a dashboard that analyzes the status of domestic loans in the United States. The original image is here: `http://data-informed.com/wp-content/uploads/2013/07/Tableau-illo-Domestic_Loan_Analysis-650x438.jpg`.

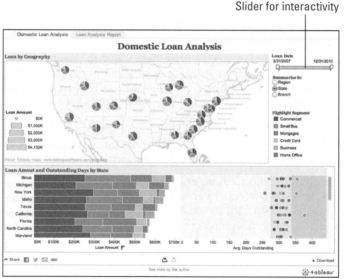

Figure 13-1: Domestic loans in the United States.

Things that work well:

- **Color consistency:** One thing that's evident throughout this visualization is the consistency of the colors in the dashboard. On the right is a single legend — Highlight Segment — that shows the legend for the color, which remains in both the bar chart at the bottom and the pie charts on the map.

- **Simplicity:** The two large charts make digesting the data easy.

- **Interactivity:** The slider in the top-right corner controls the time period displayed on the charts. That interactive feature puts users in control of what they view.

Things that don't work:

✔ **Chart choice:** The small pie charts that are overlaid on the map are of little value. They're hard to view, and without clicking every single one, the user can't determine which of them are worth evaluating. It's also virtually impossible to tell which states or regions the charts pertain to.

✔ **Color choice:** The abundant use of red, blue, and orange are misleading, especially in the stacked bar chart at the bottom of the data viz. At a glance, users may think that the colors could mean good versus bad; in fact, they're just associated with a specific segment. This type of color usage harkens back to our recommendation about being careful with the use of RAG colors (see Chapter 10). An alternative is to use more muted colors, such as a range of grays and blues.

✔ **Data overload:** There's a lot of data on the screen, but none of it really identifies the most important data or trends that users need to pay attention to. This visualization displays data for viewing instead of adding real value.

Data visualization 2

Figure 13-2 shows a data visualization of a mobility survey conducted by http://sapdashboardgallery.com. You can find the original image at www.sapdashboardgallery.com/uploads/86/FINAL.swf.

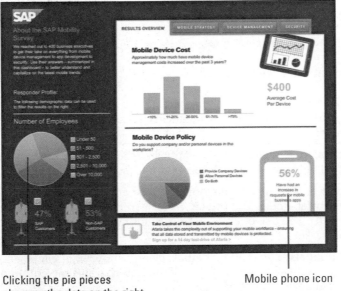

Clicking the pie pieces
changes the data on the right

Mobile phone icon

Figure 13-2: Mobility survey.

Things that work well:

- ✓ **Colors:** The colors are very safe. The dark brown background complements the colors in the charts.

- ✓ **White space:** The use of white space makes the chart data easy to read.

- ✓ **Icons:** The icons, such as the mannequins with coats and the tablet, really help emphasize that they are business owners. Notice the use of a mobile phone's outline to hold some of the statistical data.

- ✓ **Interactivity:** Allowing users to view and change the number of employees and thereby modify the data on all the charts is a nice interactive touch.

Things that don't work:

The component of this visualization that works least well is text size. Although the titles are clearly marked, the text in some areas is small, which makes it hard to read.

Don't compromise font size in the interest of adding more text. Instead, find a simpler way to add the text.

Data visualization 3

Figure 13-3 shows the SalesForce data visualization, which shows the names of the salespeople and the size of the deal they have either closed or have pending. You can view the original image here: http://eu.demo. qlikview.com/QvAJAXZfc/opendoc.htm?document=qvdocs%2FSales force.qvw&host=Demo11&anonymous=true.

Things that work well:

- ✓ **White space:** White space separates the graphical areas and text, which is especially important in a data visualization with a lot of metadata (information about the data itself).

- ✓ **Text size:** The larger fonts emphasize the most important values, which stand out from the less important information.

- ✓ **Color choice:** The legend for the color and story of the journey is very clearly labeled at the top left as past (red), present (gold), and future (green). The use of color in this visualization is understandable and consistent.

- ✓ **Text labels:** The bold text labels clearly show what each section displays. Notice the consistency of the text size and the colors of the labels at each level, from top to bottom.

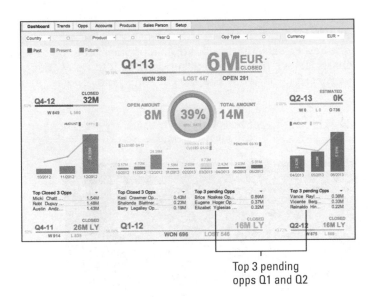

Figure 13-3: SalesForce.

Things that don't work:

- **Chart choice:** The most confusing part of this data viz is the use of charts, particularly the one in the middle. A closer look shows that the charts in the middle repeat the charts on the left and the right. Although it's clear that the author is trying to show how the past and future compare with the present, repeating charts seldom provides much value.

  Duplication is a waste of valuable real estate.

- **Cut-off text:** Notice that the names of the top-three pending "opps" are cut off. Cutting off text on a data viz can make it very hard for users to read. In a large organization, it's unlikely that everyone will be familiar with every piece of data in a visualization, such as the opportunity name in this case.

  When you follow the Business Intelligence Dashboard Formula (BIDF) blueprint, you begin by asking for the short names that you can use on the data viz. Knowing how to abbreviate terminology helps you avoid cut-off text.

- **Metadata:** The data is well laid out, but there's still a lot of it. This data viz gives a complete picture, but it's hard to determine on first viewing whether there are any real problems.

  Because there's so much metadata, it would be helpful to highlight any exceptions or areas that require the user's immediate attention.

Data visualization 4

Figure 13-4 shows a sales dashboard from a popular blog that displays high-finance charts. To see the original dashboard, visit `http://blog.mgm-tp.com/wp-content/uploads/2013/01/Dashboard.png`.

Same colors for
different pie charts

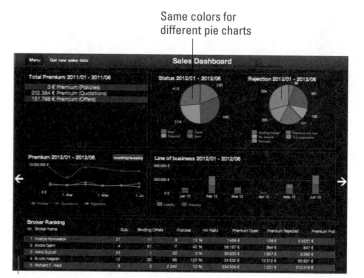

Black background

Figure 13-4: Sales dashboard.

Things that work well:

Unfortunately, we can't find much in this data viz that works very well.

Things that don't work:

- **Color choice:** Black backgrounds are tricky. Many newbies use a large dark background to make the charts stand out. Over time, however, most users get tired of the dark background, and if they have to print the data visualization, this background is surely a great waste of ink. Avoid using black or very dark backgrounds throughout a data viz unless you can overlay each section with a much lighter color. If you look back at Figure 13-2, you can see that the black background worked on that data viz because it was broken up by large amounts of white space.

- **Chart choice:** The Status pie chart on the left has four almost-equal slices and tells the user absolutely nothing. (Chapter 4 explains why pie charts can be a problem.) Using an ascending bar chart would make the small change in the values more evident.

✔ **Chart choice:** The Line of Business bar charts are tiny and hard to read. Moving the Line of Business column charts to where the line charts are currently located and increasing the height would allow more of the values to be shown. Presently it looks like it just got stuck in the corner.

Data visualization 5

Figure 13-5 shows a data visualization of a retail dashboard. See the original image here: www.bimeanalytics.com/wp-content/uploads/2012/06/bime_bigquery.png.

Filtering menu

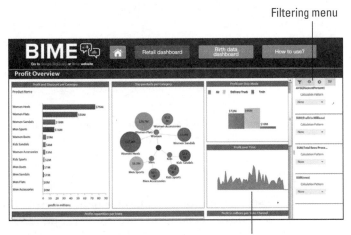

No labels on axes

Figure 13-5: Retail dashboard.

Things that work well:

✔ **White space:** The use of white space separates the graphical areas and the text.

✔ **Text labels:** Each section is well labeled, making it easy for users to understand what they're looking at. In addition, the boxes around sections help users see each section as a discrete entity.

✔ **Menu:** The filtering menu is vertical and provides an array of options that allow users to drill down into the data.

Things that don't work:

✔ **Chart choice:** The choices of charts for Top Products Per Category and Profit over Time are questionable. In addition, on the Profit over Time chart the axes are not labeled.

Instead of showing Top Products Per Category as bubbles of varying sizes, a pie chart showing the top five slices, with the remaining products grouped in an Other category, might work better. The Profit over Time chart could be represented with a simple line chart with some form of legend to help determine what the time frame is. The lack of labels on the axes of this chart limits its value. The users can't tell what the time period is or what the spread of profit is from the lowest point to the highest.

✔ **Menu filters:** Having the pull-down menus on the right side instead of the left side isn't consistent with what users expect. (See Chapter 6 for more information on the patterns in which humans digest information.)

You should never reinvent the wheel with the design of your data viz. The filtering menu should be on the left side of the page, where the user will look first.

✔ **Color choice:** There's no coordination of colors in this dashboard, and the color choices lack clarity. It appears that random colors were selected, which detracts from the overall visualization. It's very difficult to determine what's important or where to look first.

A better solution would be to use RAG colors (red, amber, green) to show trends and to use muted colors for the rest of the information. See information about RAG colors in Chapter 10.

Data visualization 6

Figure 13-6 shows a data visualization created for policy information in the insurance industry. See the original image here: `http://users.infragistics.com/tsnyder/Pomegranate_Dashboard.PNG`.

Things that work well:

✔ **Color choice:** The blue, green, and yellow color scheme is well executed. It's very easy to follow the three categories in the chart legend through-out the data viz. In addition, the white background on the left and the light blue background on the right separate the two areas nicely.

✔ **Layout:** The layout is easy to digest and doesn't crowd any of the information. Note that a subtle line divides each of the areas.

Things that don't work:

✔ **Tables:** The Pending Quote table needs more context to explain whether the quotes shown are the top five pending quotes or just the ones for that month. Their importance is vague.

✔ **Chart choice:** The stacked bar chart that shows New Policy Per Year by type is clear, although we question the value of showing the data this way. It would be more efficient to show the data in columns so that you can instantly see the different heights.

Column bars would be a better
choice than stackable bars.

Figure 13-6: Policy information.

The change from year to year seems to be so small that it might make
more sense to add some context and perhaps also display the variance
from year to year.

In addition, the Active Policy by Type 3-D doughnut chart is unnecessary and ineffective. Although we often see these types of fussy charts,
it would be more effective to use a simple pie chart.

✔ **What-if scenario:** It's not apparent how to use the slider in the Active
Policy by Type section. A simple label that explains would be quite
helpful. Also, making the 3-D doughnut chart interactive is fun the first
few times, but it distracts from the meaning of the data over the long
term.

Data visualization 7

Figure 13-7 is an example of a visualization that's overly busy. You can
find this example online at `http://makingdatameaningful.com/`
`wp-content/uploads/2013/06/Dashboards4.jpg`.

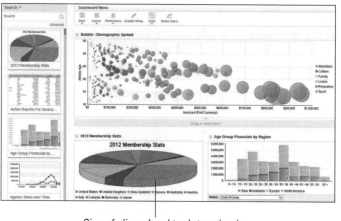

Size of slices hard to determine in
3D pie chart

Figure 13-7: Cluttered data visualization.

Things that work well:

- **Chart choice:** The bubble chart at the top clearly shows the demographic progression of the membership and is a great use of a bubble chart.

- **Sections:** Using three clear sections makes it easy for users to view the visualizations.

Things that don't work:

- **Chart choice:** This visualization shows how 3-D pie charts can get out of control. Showing 2012 Membership Stats in a 3-D horizontal pie chart is not only ineffective but also severely dilutes the message of the data because it's hard to tell what the size of the actual slices are.

  Because the sizes aren't very different, an ascending bar chart would work better so that you can more easily see the difference.

- **Color consistency:** All the charts use the same colors, but those colors have different meanings.

  As we state in Chapter 10, you need to use consistent colors to convey meaning. In this case, it would have been better to use a gradient of soft colors for the bottom charts to avoid having to reuse so many colors in different ways across each chart. The effect is quite confusing.

Data visualization 8

Figure 13-8 displays data for City Smart Meter, which monitors power consumption. See the original image here: www.informationbuilders.com/sites/all/files/images/dashboard-bam-utilities.jpg.

Icons

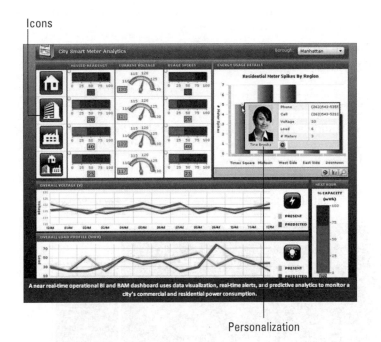

Personalization

Figure 13-8: City Smart Meter.

Things that work well:

- ✔ **Personalization:** Some people may argue that adding a friendly human face is a waste of space. In this case, the photo makes the data viz very inviting and provides information for users.

- ✔ **Icons:** The icons that show different divisions or categories are very effective. The icons not only save space but also bring to life the different types of buildings at which the power company checks meters. The same goes for the lightning icon in the Overall Voltage chart at the bottom. Again, although some people may argue that humanizing a data viz is a waste of space, it's a good thing if it's done correctly.

Things that don't work:

✔ **Color choice:** The dark red, yellow, and green used in the thermometers and the values are overkill. Restricting these colors to the thermometers would have been effective enough. When everything has an alert of some kind, nothing stands out. We also question whether using green adds any value. Sticking to a light gray would allow more focus on the red and yellow values.

✔ **Chart choice:** Thermometer bonanza! The data viz has too many thermometers; as a result, their effects are diluted.

Data visualization 9

Figure 13-9 shows a data visualization that displays sales by geography. Visit `www.componentart.com/products/dv/showcase.aspx#dashboards` to see the original image.

Tablet version   Phone version

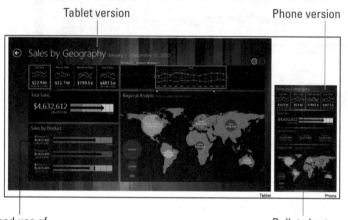

Good use of   Bullet charts
bullet charts

Figure 13-9: Sales by geography.

Note that the following things that work well and the things that don't work apply to both the tablet and phone versions in the figure.

Things that work well:

✔ **Chart choice:** The bullet charts on the left tell a clear story about how the products are selling.

✔ **Location intelligence:** The use of proportionally sized, brightly colored circles on each country makes this display fairly easy to digest.

✔ **Mobile viewing:** A great feature of this data viz is that it shows you how it will look on mobile devices. You can see a consistent layout in the two versions.

Things that don't work:

✔ **Color choice:** The striped background colors are distracting. The spectrum of colors attracts users' attention, but in the wrong direction — away from the data. A solid background would be better.

✔ **Chart choice:** The four micro line charts on the left, which show some sort of trend, add no value. Can you tell how Sales Last Year is trending by looking at the lines? Removing the lines and just displaying the numbers in large text would be much more effective. Also, the map uses a large amount of real estate compared to the value it adds.

Data visualization 10

Figure 13-10 shows a visualization of how subsidies are distributed by region in the Netherlands. The original is at

`www.tableausoftware.com/public/sites/default/files/`
`gallery/static/Screenshot_071013_025356_PM.jpg?1373494296.`

Good use of bubbles for location data

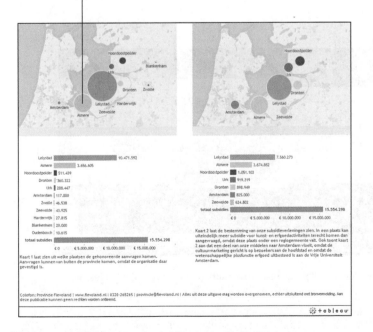

Figure 13-10: Distribution of subsidies in the Netherlands.

Things that work well:

- ✔ **Location intelligence:** The chart in this data viz is clear and narrows down a specific region. The interactive nature of this map is great for users.

- ✔ **Color choice:** The colors in the map and chart on the left have the same meaning as the colors in map and chart on the right, making it easy for users to relate the data.

Things that don't work:

- ✔ **Interactivity:** When it comes to maps, a user's first reaction typically is to click the map to see location-specific information (and to simply see if it works). The designer missed an opportunity to provide more insight by not providing any interactivity.

- ✔ **Duplication:** Because the two visualizations are identical, using a simple filter to show the data on the right in the same display as on the left would enable users to gain more value.

Data visualization 11

Figure 13-11 shows a screen shot of the Sailboats dashboard that we included on our front cover. (Image courtesy of AnalysisFactory.com.)

Stock ticker

Figure 13-11: Sailboats dashboard with all the bells and whistles.

Things that work well:

✓ **Personalization:** Although some people may consider the huge sailboat in the middle to be over the top and a bad use of real estate, the image on this executive dashboard — which was made to display on large screens and also to be used daily by executives — helps personalize the data viz. Other touches that make this data viz specific to this company are the deep blue colors and the stock ticker component. This visualization really drives home data that is on the pulse of the company's most important financial figures.

✓ **Layout:** The layout is fairly easy to digest. The charts are big and visible, and the numbers in the bottom bar are easy to read.

Things that don't work:

✓ **Noisy background:** This particular background is a bit noisy for our taste. The light blues swooshing across the back can distract from some of the charts and data in that area. A darker or solid color background would be more efficient and compete less with the charts.

✓ **Animation:** When this data viz is in action, the picture of the sailboat automatically changes every 10 seconds to scroll through five different images. Although this may be great for the big screens in the office, it's not so great for everyday use and consumption on a desktop or mobile device. A bit less animation would help to keep the user focused on the data.

There always has to be a good balance between design and functionality. Analysis Factory surely pushed the pendulum with the flashy nature of this data viz, and the users loved it. It's good to remember that your users will get attached to data visualizations that feel personalized. This data viz does that, even though we question how much real estate is consumed by the sailboat pictures. Ultimately, what's important is that the users are happy with the data viz, which was the case for this particular data viz.

Data visualization 12

Figure 13-12 shows a variation of the data visualization that was built by our BI Dashboard Formula team for a large food and beverage company. This visualization is the basis of our main example in Chapters 7 through 11.

Things that work well:

✓ **Color choice:** The muted gray color allows the alert colors to stand out.

✓ **Layout:** The layout is easy to digest as it uses a variety of circles and squares to highlight critical information. In addition, the sections are clearly labeled.

Figure 13-12: Food and beverage company sales dashboard.

Tabular data should be replaced with visuals.

Even when you try your best to stick to the guidelines we provide in this book, there are always compromises that you have to make with the business users. In the example of Figure 13-12, one of the major compromises we had to make was to include some reporting data and formatting to help the customer adapt to the experience of using visualizations. Previously, this customer had used too many reports and Excel sheets. The list of things that don't work reflects some of the compromises we had to make on the design with those users and what we hope to see them change as their environment matures.

Things that don't work:

✓ **Tables:** The entire bottom half looks like a big report, although we tried to give it a scorecard feel. In an ideal world, we would find a way to visualize the most important parts of this data instead of presenting it in tables. Also notice that we included horizontal thermometer-style charts to try to incorporate a visual aspect.

One way to improve Section b (which should be the Trends) would be to highlight the top three to five outliers in a more visual format. This could be done by using text mixed with some labeling and icons in place of the running, row-by-row format we currently have.

Recognizing Newbie Pitfalls

In This Chapter

▶ Contracting data overload syndrome

▶ Forgetting about mobile

▶ Using confusing alert colors

▶ Avoiding statistics

*A*fter training so many data viz newbies globally, we have concluded that the first encounter most of our students have with any type of data visualization is with Microsoft Excel. Excel remains the number-one business intelligence (BI) tool in the world from a market-share standpoint. Unfortunately, its flexibility often allows users to hoard tons of raw data to devise a single answer, and the problem becomes overly complex.

Data visualization is usually treated as an afterthought; it doesn't come into play until data has grown beyond the point where it can be reasonably distilled from spreadsheets and reports. Only then do people seek to understand how data visualizations can help them communicate their message effectively.

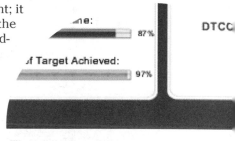

The transition from a pure reporting tool like Excel to a more advanced software visualization tool is where new users succumb to common pitfalls. In this chapter we look at pitfalls that relate to how the data is used and designed.

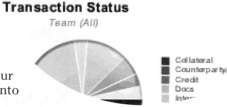

Bear the topics in this chapter in mind as you build your visualizations. As you'll discover, it's very easy to fall into one of these traps.

Going Overboard with Data

The temptation to keep adding data to any visualization is almost impossible to resist. Data overload is not only hands down the most common pitfall but also one of the hardest habits to break.

Most data visualization newbies fall into one of two categories:

- **Business analysts/super users (aka Excel addicts):** These folks love using Excel, but they usually create a monster Excel application that has reached its limit. As a result, they've been asked to simplify the application to include visuals that users can easily digest.

- **Report or data developers:** These people tend to have a deep reporting background, using tools way more advanced than Excel. When confronted with Big Data, they find that they need to simplify their message. Their users complain about the complexity of their reporting applications. In a desperate attempt to simplify, they stumble upon data visualization as the solution. They try to find ways to effectively apply visuals to their complicated systems to make them easier to digest.

If Big Data has become unmanageable, the use of visuals will help deliver true insight into the data. No set of Excel spreadsheets or reports can hold or analyze a gigabyte of data.

Like any addiction, data hoarding is hard to overcome. The first step in overcoming it is admitting that you have a problem. You can change your ways. If you haven't yet fallen into this trap, be extra-cautious going forward.

Figure 14-1 shows a first data visualization by someone who falls into one of the two preceding categories. The figure resembles a report with a few charts. Imagine trying to view a gigabyte's worth of data in this format!

Figure 14-1: An overloaded data visualization.

What can you do to stop yourself from getting sucked into the habit of adding more and more data? Here are two things to consider when you find yourself in this predicament:

- **Make sure that you spend the necessary time completing the business intelligence (BI) blueprint.** You need to work with the users to narrow down and focus on the key performance indicators and metrics that need to be tracked.

- **Create a clear message for all four sections of the blueprint.** When you have a clear idea of what story the data viz is going to tell, it's much easier to determine what combination of visuals you need to use to communicate the message effectively.

See Chapter 7 for details on developing your BI blueprint.

Don't be surprised if your users continually request a ton of unnecessary data and even rebel against displaying simplified visuals. We call this phenomenon an emotional loss of data. Users won't trust the visualization unless you present all the data for them to analyze. Curing this type of data overload usually requires a paradigm shift and retraining about how knowledge is to be shared across an organization.

Falling into the One-Shoe-Fits-All Trap

If you try to build a data visualization for everybody, absolutely nobody will use it. We call this situation the One-Shoe-Fits-All Trap.

As a data visualization newbie, your focus should be on building intelligent data visualizations with actionable data. The data visualization should have a clear story that the audience can identify. Therefore, focusing on audiences with similar needs is important.

You may be tempted to cram everything into a single data visualization for several reasons, such as a low budget, user pressure, or corporate politics. Succumbing to any of these reasons is a lose–lose situation for all parties involved. If you're in Finance, viewing Human Resources (HR) data is of no value to you, and the same applies to the HR person who now has to view Financial data. This examples illustrates why choosing related audiences is so important.

One exception to this rule occurs when you're building visualizations for a C-level audience — such as a CEO, the CEO's direct staff, or a board of directors. Those people need to see a summarized view of all the divisions in an organization on a daily basis. In this case, it's normal to have separate areas or tabs for Sales, HR, Finance, Information Technology, and so on.

To duck this trap, be sure to follow the storyboard model prescribed in Chapter 7. It ensures that you always tell a story that's unique to your audience, which is the key to long-term user adoption. If you don't craft your story for your specific audience, your users will resent you and your product for wasting their time with information that's irrelevant to them.

Focusing on the Tool Instead of the Story

You may notice that in several chapters of this book, we emphasize that you do *not* build a data visualization based on the functionality of a specific tool. When the tool is more important to you than the story, you find yourself saying "No" or "I can't" too often, and you also find your users and future projects disappearing. For in-depth information about choosing a tool, see Chapter 3.

Business users have zero interest in what you can't do. The key to success is focusing on their needs and then deciding, based on your own research, which tool is the best fit. You have many tools to choose among, and new tools are always entering this growing market. Finding the right tool may not be as hard as you think.

If you're looking for suggestions, just do an Internet search for *business intelligence data visualization tools,* and you'll find an expansive list of tools to try.

If you can't build a data viz because you can't do it with a particular tool, the business user will pay someone else to do it — or attempt to do it himself. Don't let this happen to you.

Users won't wait for approval

In the past, if you were in an enterprise environment, your technology (IT) department probably wanted to approve any new tools to be used. Many organizations required you to go through months of compliance investigations before you could adopt any new technology — even a cheap one.

But gone are the days when users patiently waited for their IT departments to perform time-consuming investigations of organizational compliance before adopting a new technology.

The fast pace of the business world, combined with the accessibility of mobile devices, has left this archaic practice in the dust. The last thing you want to do is lose your users as they wait for a tool to be chosen.

As you gather requirements, make sure that you are simultaneously working on choosing the right tool in the background, away from your users. They'll thank you for being open-minded and delivering the best possible tool to meet their needs.

Building Mobile Last

Let's face it: If you're not thinking mobile, you're probably in the wrong industry. Smartphones and tablets have forever changed the way that humans expect to interact with applications. The iTunes and Google Play stores are full of shiny, well-designed, interactive apps. They cause users to want all data visualizations to be accessible via mobile devices and to look and feel like apps.

Figure 14-2 shows a complex data viz that would be very hard to navigate on a mobile device because of the amount of information and the numerous drill-down menus. (You can find this visualization at `www.dashboardinsight.com/CMS/627c6149-6dfd-432c-9b12-d6b6aa578084/Screen%20shot%20Analyzer%20Dasboard.png`.) Figure 14-3, on the other hand, shows a simplified but easy-to-digest and clear data viz that was built with mobile devices in mind. Notice the great use of white space, text, and location intelligence. (You can see this image at `http://data-ink.com/wp-content/uploads/2013/06/dashboard_sample_mobile.jpg`.)

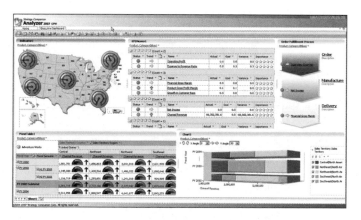

Figure 14-2: This data viz is not designed for mobile devices.

Figure 14-3: This data viz is mobile ready.

You need to have a mobile-first mindset when you're developing a data visualization. You should do several things:

- ✔ **Make it intuitive.** One thing that we all love about apps is that we don't have to read a manual before using them. Be sure to carry this same experience over to your data visualizations on mobile devices. By using visual cues and clever treatments of colors, fonts, and textures, you make your data visualization easy to digest on a desktop computer or a mobile device.

- ✔ **Account for reduced design space.** The average mobile device today is 3 to 10 inches (length and width), which represents a loss of almost half the screen real estate available on desktops. To work on mobile devices, your data visualization must take reduced screen size into consideration with regard to fonts, menus, and overall display. Smaller devices force you to develop concise data visualizations that convey your points quickly and clearly.

- ✔ **Use native mobile functionality.** Have you ever noticed that when you open an app on a mobile device and tap a menu, the specific menu for that device pops up? Be sure that all the menu options that you use in your data visualizations — be they drop-down menus or combo boxes — are compatible with all the mobile devices that your users may have. The last thing you want is for a user to get frustrated trying to use a data viz that doesn't work well on his device.

✓ **Enable sharing and social collaboration.** Social collaboration is the name of the game in the 21st century. Your users expect to have an easy and intuitive way to share their data visualization findings with others. Be sure to make this capability native and not an afterthought.

✓ **Make data quality a priority.** When your users can access your data visualizations at any time, from any place, it's important to ensure that your data visualization always outputs quality data. There's a high chance that if the system is outputting garbage data, one of your users will detect that problem before you do.

✓ **Be flexible.** Part of the appeal of mobile apps is their interactivity, clean design, and capability to adapt quickly to new requirements. It is important that you develop or choose a mobile tool for your visualization that you can easily adapt to your users' needs.

✓ **Plan for BYOD (Bring Your Own Device).** As policing the use of devices becomes a daunting task for IT, many companies are resorting to allowing their users to use their own devices in the workplace. When you're planning a data visualization, plan so that the data viz will work on the most common devices on the market: iOS devices, Android devices, and BlackBerry.

Abusing Pie Charts

There is a lot of controversy in the data-viz world about the efficacy of pie charts. Seasoned data-viz designers often look down on pie charts and believe that there are more effective ways to show the kind of data that is often displayed in a pie chart.

New data-viz designers love pie charts because they are simple to execute and easy to understand. However, you should never select a chart or graph type only because you are familiar with it. You need to make sure that you are choosing the best chart for the job. Be aware of the pie-chart trap.

Using Green for Alerts

A highly debated topic in the data visualization world is the use of green for alerts in Big Data visualizations. Most alerts, however, track negative events. As in the traffic-light scenario, red, yellow, and green are often used to signify the status of a specific event. Table 14-1 lists the most common RAG colors.

Table 14-1	Alert Colors
Color	*Use*
Red	Indicates a serious problem that requires action
Yellow	Indicates an imminent change to green or red status
Green	Provides information but doesn't require user action

Chapter 7 covers how to use the business intelligence (BI) blueprint to gather user data requirements. As part of that process, you ask the user to define the thresholds at which a metric should display an alert.

The general consensus is that red alerts are very effective at capturing readers' attention and that green alerts are a waste of space.

Figure 14-4 shows a visual dashboard that uses both red and green alerts. Notice how difficult it is to focus on the red alerts, which are overshadowed by the green areas. You can find the original image at `http://support.signagelive.com/entries/20036752-Understanding-your-Network-Dashboard`.

Figure 14-4: The green alerts in this data viz are a waste of space.

Constantly displaying green alerts dilutes the message that urgent action is needed for a metric; it also makes it hard for the reader to distinguish between what's good and what's bad without deeper analysis.

Use only red or yellow for alerts, and display everything else in a neutral color such as gray so that the alerts stand out at a glance.

Figure 14-5 shows a good example of how to include a High Risk button that shows the red alerts on the BI dashboard when the user clicks it. This makes it easy to focus the reader's attention on the events that require immediate action.

Click to see all red alerts

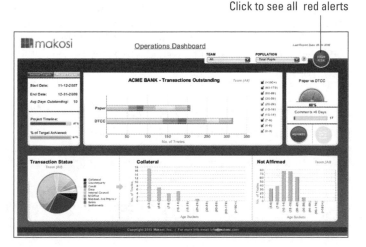

Figure 14-5: This BI dashboard includes a button to enable the user to view only red alerts.

We call green alerts in data visualizations *happy* because they give users a false sense of peace even when the most important measurements are red.

Many users insist on displaying green alerts because they believe that a Big Data visualization that displays only red is depressing, negative, or unhappy. Try to make it clear that your goal is to make the data as easy to digest as possible. You want to display only actionable data to reduce the time it takes users to focus their attention.

Ignoring Basic Statistics

We realize that the word *statistics* may evoke fear in some newbies, but we can't ignore this topic, lest we overlook one of the most powerful ways to gain true insight and value from Big Data.

Statistics is the practice or science of collecting numerical data in large quantities. We're not recommending that you go out and become a data scientist (a term used for statisticians who are also data geeks in disguise and who usually hold some type of advanced degree, such as a PhD). You may want to consider picking up a Statistics 101 book or class, however, if you have any interest.

Statistical formulas such as probability, variance, and forecast are popular today. They're fairly easy to apply to any data set, and most readers will clearly understand them. You can incorporate some of these statistical formulas into your Big Data visualizations to provide true value to users by using the techniques discussed in the following sections.

Knowing the probability that an event will occur

One statistical formula that you may be familiar with is *probability* — the likelihood or chance that an event may occur. The following formula calculates basic probability for a linear scenario. (Nonlinear scenarios are a bit complex and too much of an undertaking for a newbie.)

> Probability = Probability an Event Will Occur / Number of Possible Outcomes

On a storyboard (refer to Chapter 7), a perfect place to insert the probability is Section 1: Current State. The idea is to give users a quick overview showing whether they're likely to hit their goal.

Figure 14-6 shows a probability with some alert colors added to make the message easy to read and, most important, to clearly indicate that immediate action is needed.

Figure 14-6: Adding alert colors.

Probabilities provide a quick reality check and set the overall tone for the story the data visualization will be providing during a given period (day, week, quarter, and so on).

Applying variance to show the magnitude of change

Another popular statistical measure is *variance,* which is the difference between a set of data points.

The most commonly used formula for calculating variance is

Variance = Final Desired − Current State

Whether the output displayed is a whole number or percentage, the formula shows the magnitude of change between the beginning state and the ending state of a data point.

Displaying the variance is always a quick win and a great substitute for the line/bar chart combo, which is how the variance relationship is displayed in most visualizations. Compare Figure 14-7 and Figure 14-8 to see how much more effective a visualization can be with a plotted variance.

The chart in Figure 14-7 shows a line/bar chart combo that lets the user decipher the variance for each month. The original image is at `http://peltiertech.com/images/2009-11/BarLine_ColumnLine.png`.

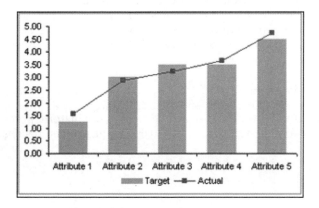

Figure 14-7: The user has to determine variance.

The second chart, shown in Figure 14-8, clearly plots the variance and takes all the guesswork out of the visual. You can find the original image at `http://ksrowell.com/blog-visualizing-data/2013/02/14/how-to-make-a-deviation-graph`.

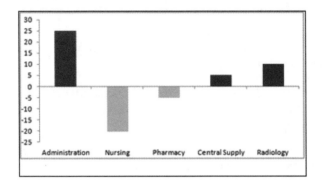

Figure 14-8: Variance is clearly displayed.

Forecasting the future

Yet another popular statistical formula that you may be familiar with is the *forecast,* which is the act of predicting or estimating an event or trend. For more details about forecasts, see Chapter 7.

When you calculate a forecast, you're really using a certain amount of historic data to predict behavior, a specific event, or a trend. For example, you could calculate the sales for the year based on the historic fact that January, usually accounts for 5 percent of the sales. If you made $500 in sales in January, you would use the following formula to forecast how much sales you can anticipate for the year:

$$\$500 / .05 = \$10,000$$

In this equation, $500 is the sales in January; .05 is the historic percentage of sales that January accounts for; and $10,000 is the projected sales for the year.

Figure 14-9 shows how forecasts are displayed in most data visualizations as a simple line in a chart. (This image is from `www.exactsoftware.com/docs/DocBinBlob.aspx?ID=%7B67d0ec85-71ae-4188-9646-13831136cc53%7D`.) Forecasts indicate how a given activity may perform in the future.

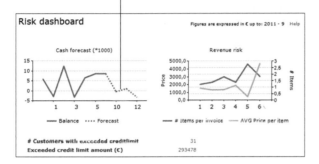

Displayed as a simple line on a chart

Figure 14-9: This typical display of a forecast line shows that cash flow will eventually become an issue for this organization.

Changing the future with predictive analysis

Forecasts have been used for decades. With the introduction of Big Data, however, the field of predictive analysis is being invigorated. In predictive analysis, you take the data you have and make authoritative decisions about what the data means and how it can be applied to improve something.

Most organizations are finally realizing that the best ways to use Big Data are to react to events and to prevent them. For example, if you get data about the failure rate from an assembly line part, you can use that to predict when to change that part instead of waiting for it to fail. You become proactive instead of reactive.

The insights generated by predictive analysis often produce return on investment data that you can provide to your organization. Think of using predictive data as providing an option to change the future.

Not Mastering User Engagement

If you build a data visualization, but it doesn't engage the interest of your audience, all your work is for naught. User engagement throughout the development process is the key to success.

Problems with user engagement usually take one of these forms:

- ✔ **No user engagement:** Lack of user engagement is the most common scenario. Data visualization developers go off into a dark corner to gather requirements and create; then they pop up later with something that the user is unhappy with. We call this situation the "nuclear bomb." The data viz is built delicately and secretly, but when it's finally presented, the effect is like a destructive explosion.

- ✔ **Too much user engagement:** The other extreme is too much user engagement — particularly when you lose control of the conversation and get a never-ending list of change requests from your users.

To avoid both of these problems, follow the steps in Chapters 7 and 8 for developing your story, creating your first storyboard, and creating your mockup.

Some other key elements may help you strike the right balance with your users. When you have the appropriate amount of user engagement, you can gain your users' trust, maintain it, and deliver a big data visualization that exceeds their expectations.

Table 14-2 lists some ways to engage users. These techniques go a long way toward building trust and credibility.

Table 14-2	Ways to Engage Your Users	
Technique	**Description**	**Result**
Promptness	Respect start and end times for meetings and the project. Doing so goes a long way to keeping your users engaged long-term.	Users view you and the development process as being professional.
Focus	Ensure that all meetings stay focused.	Users perceive you as being in control of the situation.

Technique	Description	Result
Organization	Set an agenda for meetings, and stick to it. If you say that you're going to show users something, have it ready for viewing as promised.	Users recognize that you have a high level of professionalism and are serious about your tasks.
Productivity	Ensure that all goals are accomplished within the allotted time.	Users will be willing to return to you for future data visualization projects.
Appearance	When meeting your audience, dress professionally, and be ready to conduct business.	Users view you as a senior resource who has more authority than lower-level colleagues.

Part V
The Part of Tens

For more Parts of Tens, download our article "Top Ten Blunders to Avoid When Creating a Data Visualization." You can find it at www.dummies.com/extras/datavisualization.

In this part . . .

✔ Find out about ten great data viz resources you should book-mark. You'll find valuable information from experts who provide their own unique perspective on data visualization as well as examples of wells-executed data viz.

✔ Look at the top ten fears of data viz newbies. This chapter will help you identify fears you have so that you can avoid letting them hold you back.

15

Top Ten Data Visualization Resources

In This Chapter

▶ Discovering infographics submitted by user groups

▶ Learning about data viz from experts

▶ Adding skills to your data viz toolkit

The Internet is full of data visualizations. Some are great, some are less than great, and some are awful. Because of the popularity of infographics and other visuals, it seems that almost everyone wants to try his or her hand at data visualization.

We encourage you to experiment in the world of data visualization. We want you to use data visualizations to help your data tell interesting stories and provide a competitive advantage. But before you create a data viz, we suggest that you look at the excellent examples shown in the resources suggested in this chapter. For ongoing inspiration, bookmark the sites in your browser, and check them out on a regular basis. New trends and information are being shared daily.

J2.142 Pageviews
Dec 1, 2006 - Dec 31, 2006: 53,855 (1

00:03:22 Avg. Time on Si
Dec 1, 2006 - Dec 31, 2006: 00:03:31 (

50.44% % New Visits
Dec 1, 2006 - Dec 31, 2006: 49.73% (1

Map Overlay world

Edward Tufte

www.edwardtufte.com/tufte

Yale University Professor Edward Tufte's views on data visualization have helped shape the industry. He provides compelling discussions and insights through his blog and his always-sold-out courses. We are big fans! Mico owns all his books, and Stephanie attended his course.

Visual.ly

http://visual.ly

The Visual.ly site is 100 percent infographics. Whether you want to have the company create one for you or you want to pore over the vast collection, this site has something for everyone. You can use the database to search by topic or industry, such as animals, technology, social media, and geography. It's great for inspiration, creativity, and brainstorming.

The Functional Art

www.thefunctionalart.com

The Functional Art is a great blog that's an outgrowth of the book of the same name by University of Miami (Mico's alma mater) Professor Albert Cairo. Cairo has an active online presence. He provides insight and classes that help newbies take their data viz skills to the next level.

Visualizing Data

http://hbr.org/special-collections/insight/visualizing-data

The diverse Visualizing Data blog on the Harvard Business Review site covers the most important topics relating to data visualization, including when you shouldn't use data viz and whether you are getting enough value from the data viz you created. You'll always find insightful and thought-provoking points of view, and you'll learn from some of the most brilliant minds in the field.

Chart Porn

http://chartporn.org

Chart Porn is a great site with a provocative name and lots of inspiring examples of data visualizations. It offers data visualizations based on global topics and trends. As the racy title implies, the site provides some amazing examples of charts, infographics, and maps.

The Excel Charts Blog

www.excelcharts.com/blog

Jorge Camos has done a great job of providing free tutorials, discussions, and best practices for creating data visualizations in Microsoft Excel. His blog is a great Excel resource for newbies and introduces you to best practices.

FlowingData

http://flowingdata.com

You'll never get bored with Nathan Yau's perspective on data; he hovers between data scientist and graphic designer. On his FlowingData site, he writes with humor and clear opinions on the data visualization industry. (Some content is available to the general public, but you have to have a subscription to be able to access everything the site offers.) He also has several excellent books on the market, and his blog provides great real-world examples of data visualizations.

Datavisualization.ch

http://datavisualization.ch/events

You can find a useful list of top data viz events around the world here. This site is great for those who want to dive a bit deeper and meet like-minded people.

GE Data Visualization

http://visualization.geblogs.com

As one of the biggest companies in the world, General Electric (GE) uses its data viz site to show the world how it operates and gives examples from a variety of different fields. The data visualizations are fascinating, and they help the company showcase its successes. Kudos to GE for riding the front of the data viz wave.

#dataviz and #bigdata

```
https://twitter.com/search?q=dataviz&src=typd
```

You can find some of the best, most up-to-date resources and information about data viz by tracking the #dataviz hashtag on Twitter. The same goes for #bigdata. You'll often see tweets by some of the other resources listed in this chapter.

Top Ten Fears of New Data-Viz Creators

W e know that you're very interested in finding out how to create great data visualizations. If you weren't, you wouldn't be reading this book. But admit it: You're also a bit scared. There's no shame in that. As newbies, we were a bit overwhelmed when we created our first data visualizations. Tackling something new is always unsettling. Often, a lot is riding on producing a data viz that people find useful.

So how can you conquer these fears? The best way is to face them, and we want to help. This chapter looks at the top ten fears you may have as you start your first data viz.

We've worked with data viz clients for several years, and the same fears come up time and time again. We hope this list will show you that you're on the right track and among friends. Just jump in and get started — after reading this chapter.

Telling the Wrong Story

You've heard that data viz is about storytelling. Good data visualizations tell important stories that generate fabulous insights, right? But as you start developing your data viz, you have no idea what story you're going to tell. You can't know what the story is until you get everything assembled and put in place. So fear rears its ugly head. You wonder, "What if I don't have a story to tell? What if it's not inspiring and compelling?"

First things first. You can't tell your story until you know what the data says, and you can't know what the data says until you figure out what data you will use. You need to start at the beginning and put all the elements together. Your first step is to figure out what questions you want to answer. For step-by-step guidelines, see Chapter 4. When you have all your preparation done, you'll feel less overwhelmed and ready to make story choices.

Creating an Ugly Data Viz

One major reason why data visualizations have become so popular is that they look great online and make a big splash. Think about the ones you've seen that have really made an impression on you. Starting with the idea that you'll create a great-looking data viz too, however, only amplifies the anxiety you feel.

Ugly data visualizations are just as useless as beautiful ones that have no meaning. It's true that people will judge the quality of your data viz by its design. As visual beings, we respond to images. If a data viz has no real value apart from being eye candy, users won't continue to use it. For this reason, your first goal is to answer the questions you and your stakeholders have about the data. After you've done that, you can concern yourself with the visual aspects.

Picking the Wrong Things to Measure

You may think that if you choose to include the company's current key performance indicators (KPIs) in the data viz, you can't go too far wrong. That's partially true, but there's much more to it than that, and that's what concerns you. You know that the KPIs will include some of the right data, but what about all the other measures that your department cares about? And if your department (or the client) doesn't have KPIs, how should you proceed?

One way is to begin by understanding what the data viz will accomplish. Will it answer questions about how the sales force is performing? Will it try to show which territories are generating the most revenue? After you decide what the purpose of your data viz will be, try to agree on a title for it. That title likely won't be the final one. Lots of things can happen during the project's duration to change it. But at least you can see whether everyone is in agreement at the beginning about where you're headed. After you've picked the title, ask everyone to agree on the measures that should be used to fulfill the promise of the title. If you get a dialogue started, you are moving forward in an intelligent way.

Alienating Other Stakeholders

You may be alienating other data viz stakeholders by speaking your mind. How can this be? You want to do your best for your collaborators and your company, but you find that you just don't agree with their ideas about the data viz. You wonder whether you should speak up and risk their disapproval. The answer probably is yes.

Voicing your ideas about how to proceed can make your data viz stronger. It's also important to hear what your colleagues have to say. You want to be aware if someone has a vested interest in a particular outcome. If you determine that someone does have a bias, you should speak to them about how it might affect the outcome. On the other hand, someone may have a different viewpoint that's worth considering. Either way, don't be afraid to speak your mind, and encourage others to do the same. You can be sure that your managers will voice their opinions when the data viz is presented to them. Then you'll wish that you'd considered all the angles; otherwise, you may appear to be unprepared to answer questions and may fail to demonstrate that you understand the data.

Misunderstanding the Audience for Your Data Viz

You may think that you know the audience for your data viz. If you have an internal audience, you believe that you know what the users want. You do your homework and speak to all the major stakeholders. You want to have a clear vision of users' expectations and work to understand how they intend to use the data viz.

If you have an external audience, you do your best to research who your users are and what they need. But you still have a nagging feeling that you haven't connected with all the groups who will use your data viz. This fear isn't unfounded. It's possible that you can miss speaking to someone who will use your data viz. You can rectify this problem by asking all your major stakeholders to use the data visualization for several days as a pretest. A data viz isn't set in stone; you can modify it. By pretesting, you can gain confidence that you have hit your target.

Forgetting about Copyrights and Legal Matters

When you set out to create a data viz, it's unlikely that your first thought is about legal considerations. Your focus probably is on taking massive amounts of data and turning it into useful information. (Your corporate lawyers would be disappointed if they knew that.) When you've completed the task of creating your data viz, however, your thoughts do turn to the legal aspects, and you may feel intimidated.

If you know a few simple rules, you can feel more confident that you're taking the right actions to protect your company:

- **Put a copyright date and your company's name at the bottom of the data viz.** You may think that this is unnecessary for an internal audience, but just in case the data viz finds its way outside the company, you should put in the copyright.

- **Set out the terms and conditions that users of the data viz must adhere to.** If you're unsure what's required, ask your manager. You can find more detail about copyrights, terms, and conditions in Chapter 11.

Selecting the Wrong Tool

If you're a newbie, one of the following descriptions probably applies to you:

- You aren't sure what tool to use, and your anxiety is sky-high.

- You've used a simple tool like Microsoft Excel in the past, and you want to step up your game and use something more powerful, but you aren't sure what tool fits the bill.

- You've fallen in love with a specific data viz tool because you've seen others use it, but you have no experience with it.

In all these cases, you have valid concerns. They all involve learning something new. You wonder whether you're up to the task. The answer is yes, but you need to know how to go about selecting the right tool. The good news is that there's a rule of thumb. The key to picking the right tool is picking it last — after all the data preparation is done.

This idea may make you uncomfortable, because you want to know everything you're going to do before you begin a new data viz. But picking the right tool is akin to picking the right chart (see the next section): You need to know what data you want to display before selecting a chart type. Each tool has its own positives and negatives. You want to choose a tool that fits with your capabilities, goals, and data. For some ideas, see Chapter 3.

Making the Wrong Chart Choices

Choosing the right chart to display your data greatly influences the value of your completed data viz. Chapter 13 includes some examples of poor chart choices. From looking at these examples, you see that the use of the right chart can make or break a data viz.

To avoid making the wrong choice, it's best to try a few options with live data. Sometimes, the only way to find out what works is to experiment.

 To make choosing the right chart less baffling, presentation expert Dr. Andrew V. Abela, chairman of the School of Business and Economics at The Catholic University of America, created a "chart chooser" that you can use to help facilitate your choice. You can find it at `http://extremepresentation.typepad.com/blog/2006/09/choosing_a_good.html`. It helps you match your situation with the right chart.

Picking Bad/Noncomplementary Colors

If you fear choosing the right colors for your data viz, you're in good company. This fear is ever-present in new data-viz creators. You're likely to find selecting colors for your data viz daunting, because it's no easy feat to pick the right colors. You can use online tools to help you make color choices, however. See Chapter 10 for details about those tools.

 Some colors have a meaning, and you need to be aware of them. The RAG (red, amber, green) colors, for example, are the same colors used for traffic lights. Because most users are familiar with stoplights, they intuitively recognize that red means "stop," amber means "caution," and green means "go." When you use these colors in a data viz, your users apply what they already know about them to the information you're presenting. Consequently, if you want to alert them to something that requires attention, make sure to use red, not purple or blue.

 Also, some people are color-blind. For genetic reasons, they don't see colors quite the same way that others do. For this reason, don't get carried away with wild colors. Your best bet is to choose colors with which everyone is familiar. Leave the fancy stuff to the designers.

Using Too Much Data

Feeling that you're inundated with data can make you fearful that you're displaying too much data. You want to get to the heart of the matter and eliminate extraneous data, but you don't want to eliminate any data that could be valuable. So you wonder what data you should choose and how much of it you should include.

Displaying too much data in your data viz is definitely a concern. You want to start with the minimum amount of data and add more as necessary. Examples sprinkled throughout the book illustrate how messy things get when a visualization has too much data. You want to show as much as you can so that users can gain serendipitous insights, but you have to make sure that you're not obscuring the most important insights. Displaying too much data can cause confusion. If you have more data than you can use in one data viz, perhaps it's wise to create another data viz for that data.

Index

• A •

A List Apart (website), 76
abbreviations, 179
Abela, Andrew V. (professor and
    consultant), 217
accessibility
  FAQ sections, 153
  mobile design, 133, 195
  scalable systems, 10
  user adoption, importance to, 11, 166
accuracy
  infographics, 23
  perceptions, 164
  what-if scenarios, ramifications, 129
actionable data. *See also* data overload
  forecasting, 95
  software features, 36
  storyboard content, selecting, 86
  user impact, 93, 94, 199
"Advanced Data Visualization (ADV)
    Platforms" (Evelson and Yuhanna), 35
aesthetics. *See also* visuals
  data visualizations, compared to
      infographics, 14
  forcing data to fit, 17, 20, 51
  importance, 10, 166
  mobile design, importance to, 131
  ugly visualizations, fear of, 214
  valueless without effective data, 109
  white space, 74, 142, 173, 180–181, 195
alert colors, RAG (red, amber, green)
  connotation, 56, 74, 144–145, 158, 217
  financial sector use, 61
  green, misuse, 197–199
  lending clarity, example, 182
  misleading, example, 177
alerts
  dashboards, 22
  exceptions, 112–113
  green, misleading use of, 197–199
  red, misleading use of, 74
  sparing use, 186
  stakeholder notifications, 36
  text analysis statements, 62
  visual cues, 157–158
all-caps text, 59
amber
  "caution" connotation, 56, 61, 145, 217
  contrast, need for, 116
analysis, trends
  marketing campaign performance,
      123–125
  patterns, 18, 121–122
  representation techniques, 119–120
  storyboards, 92–94
Analysis Factory (website), 188
animations, merits, 36
appeal, visual
  data visualizations, compared to
      infographics, 14
  importance, 10, 166
  mobile design, importance to, 131
  ugly visualizations, fear of, 214
  valueless without effective data, 109
  white space, 74, 142, 173, 180–181, 195
  worthless without information, 23
"Apple's 6 Simple Rules for Designing a
    Killer iOS App" (Pachal), 77
apps, design
  benefits, 132–133
  data overload, 42
  device-independent accessibility, 166
  example, 186–187
  guidelines, 175
  intuitive interfaces, 166, 196
  location intelligence, 158–159
  mobile-first mindset, 195–197
  responsive design principles, 76–77
  visual appeal, 131
arrows, 139
aspect ratio, defined, 77

attention spans
  high-impact data, 94
  KPI counts, 84
  load times, 166–167
  storytelling for shortened, 81
attractiveness. *See also* visuals
  data visualizations, compared to
      infographics, 14
  forcing data to fit, 17, 20, 51
  importance, 10, 166
  mobile design, importance to, 131
  ugly visualizations, fear of, 214
  valueless without effective data, 109
  white space, 74, 142, 173, 180–181, 195
audience, focus group. *See also*
      humanization; user adoption (UA)
  attention spans, 81, 84, 94, 166–167
  colors, mock-ups, 99, 100, 199
  common actions, 134
  communication, 215
  emotional loss of data, 193
  executives, 84, 101
  goals, 84, 87–89
  KPIs, 89–91
  super users, 89, 152, 192
  types, 85–86
  user engagement, 204–205
availability, 24/7, 166

• *B* •

background, Gestalt theory, 71
background color
  dark, 142, 180
  distracting, 187, 189
  separating elements, 182
Backupify (website), 19
balance, pattern design, 74
Balsamiq Mockups (website), 75, 104
bar charts, 44, 201
beginner(s)
  color choices, safe, 56, 139–145
  fears, 71, 213–218
  pencil and paper, advantages, 102
beginner mistakes
  chart selection, 49
  color choices, 60, 139, 180
  data overload, 93, 192–193

display of unnecessary data, 93
focus group management, 99
green, misuse as alert color, 197–199. *See also* RAG (red, amber, green) colors
inaccurate what-if recommendations, 129
mobile design, neglected, 195–197
One-Shoe-Fits-All Trap, 85, 193–194
pie-chart overuse, 197
statistics, lack of familiarity, 200–203
tool dependence, 194
user engagement, lack of mastery, 204–205
visualization as afterthought, 191
Behance (website), 140
BI (Business Intelligence)
  failure and user adoption barriers, 161–162
  importance, 8
  Microsoft Excel, overuse, 191, 192
  overview, 82
  what-if practice, traditional compared to BIDF, 90
BI Brainz, 9
bias, 35, 215
BIDF (Business Intelligence Dashboard Formula). *See also* mock-ups; storyboards
  Blueprint (website), 90
  mock-ups, Blueprint, 115–118, 121–125, 128
  narrow data focus, Blueprint, 193
  overview, 10
  storyboard sections, 83
  website, 148
  what-if practice, traditional BI compared to BIDF, 90
BIDF BI Blueprint
  abbreviations, identifying, 179
  alert thresholds, 198
  data overload, avoiding, 193
  mock-ups, 115–118, 121–125, 128
  website, 90
Big Data. *See also* data overload
  challenges, 32
  collection, 33–34
  definition, 7, 29–30
  Four Vs, 32
  insight, valuable, 95, 113

mock-ups, importance of, 100
pie charts, 47
predictive analysis, 203
QlikView software, 37
quality control, 34–35
real-time, 154
sources, 30
Tableau software, 36–37
tool evaluation, 35–36
unstructured content, 33–34
uses, 30–31
value, 34–35
#bigdata Twitter hashtag, 212
big-picture considerations, 173
BIME Analytics (website), 181
BIScorecard (website), 161
black and white, for mock-ups, 100–101
black backgrounds, 142, 180
Blueprint, BIDF BI
  abbreviations, identifying, 179
  alert thresholds, 198
  data overload, avoiding, 193
  mock-ups, 115–118, 121–125, 128
  website, 90
body, layout, 148
Boston University (website), 119
Bring Your Own Device (BYOD), 197
bubble charts, examples, 184, 187
business
  Big Data, uses, 30–31
  challenges, 32
  customer information, 33–34
  insight, better than hindsight, 113
  stakeholder notification alerts,
    visualization tools, 36
  techniques for success, 194, 204–205
Business Intelligence (BI)
  failure and user adoption barriers, 161–162
  importance, 8
  Microsoft Excel, overuse, 191, 192
  overview, 82
  what-if practice, traditional compared to
    BIDF, 90
Business Intelligence Dashboard Formula
    (BIDF). *See also* mock-ups; storyboards
  Blueprint (website), 90

mock-ups, Blueprint, 115–118,
    121–125, 128
narrow data focus, Blueprint, 193
overview, 10
storyboard sections, 83
website, 148
what-if practice, traditional BI compared
    to BIDF, 90
Business Intelligence Dashboard Formula
    Business Intelligence (BIDF BI)
    Blueprint
  abbreviations, identifying, 179
  alert thresholds, 198
  data overload, avoiding, 193
  mock-ups, 115–118, 121–125, 128
  website, 90
BYOD (Bring Your Own Device), 197

● *C* ●

calls to action, 157
Camos, Jorge (blogger)
  Excel Charts Blog, 211
candlestick charts, 49–51
capital letters, 59
Carland: A century of motoring in America
    infographic (website), 14
case study infographics, 23
Chart Porn (website), 210
ChartGizmo (website), 49
ChartGo (website), 49
charts
  alternatives to, 47–48
  appropriateness to data, 112
  bar, 44, 201
  bubble, 184, 187
  candlestick, misuse, 49–50, 51
  choice guidelines, 173
  flow charts, 17
  maps, compared to, 159
  online tools, 49
  radar, misuse, 49, 50, 51
  selection, 41–43
  simple, 44–45
  waterfall, misuse, 50–51
  wrong, fear of choosing, 217

charts, pie
  controversy, 44, 197
  limitations, 112
  misuse, 45–47
checklists, 16
chronologies, 16, 23, 24
clarity, 110–111
closure, Gestalt theory, 69–70
cognitive science
  Gestalt theory, 67–71
  visual patterns, 71–74
collaboration. *See also* focus groups;
      social media
  design tools, 102–103
  disagreements, 215
  impact on user adoption, 161
  interactivity benefits, 18
  link sharing, 151
  mobile design, 133, 197
  mock-ups, 103
color
  anxiety, 139, 217
  charts, 42
  company branding guidelines,
      139–142
  consistency, 60, 173, 184
  guidelines, 173
  infographics, 23
  mock-ups, black and white, 100–101
  pattern design, 74
  scheme creation, 142–144
  subjectivity, 132
  text, 56, 60–61
color, background
  dark, 142, 180
  distracting, 187, 189
  separating elements, 182
color blindness, 217
Color Scheme Designer (website), 143
colors, RAG (red, amber, green)
  connotation, 56, 74, 144–145, 158, 217
  financial sector use, 61
  green, misuse, 197–199

  lending clarity, example, 182
  misleading, example, 177
column charts, 44
comparison infographics, 24, 25
compilation infographics, 24
Component Art (website), 186
components, visual
  correlations, clarity, 111
  device compatibility, 196
  footers, 148, 155, 156
  headers, 148, 152
  help menus, 106
  horizontal tab sets, 138
  icons, 139, 151, 153, 174
  labels, 42, 43, 56–60, 174
  links, 147–153
  logos, 106
  menu selectors, 134, 136–138
  menus, guidelines, 77, 132, 175, 196
  overlapping, 174
  placement patterns, 71–74
  templates, 16, 74–75, 105–107
  text, 55–61, 174
  titles, 57, 106, 164–165
  vertical tab sets, 138
  visual cues, 156–158
compromises, 190
conditional formatting
  exceptions, 112–113
  sparing use, 186
  text analysis statements, 62
  visual cues, 157–158
conditional formatting, RAG (red, amber,
      green) colors
  connotation, 56, 74, 144–145, 158, 217
  financial sector use, 61
  green, misuse, 197–199
  lending clarity, example, 182
  misleading, example, 177
Connor, Marcia (consultant), 29
consistency
  branding guidelines, 139–142
  color, 60, 173, 184

evaluating text, 174
mobile device design, 75–77
text sizes, 59
content design, mobile
benefits, 132–133
data overload, 42
device-independent accessibility, 166
example, 186–187
guidelines, 175
mobile-first mindset, 195–197
responsive design principles, 76–77
visual appeal, 131
content types, 16–17
context
colors, 60–61
definition, 35
fonts, 58–60
importance, 53–54
labels, 56–57
metadata, 173
text, 55–58, 174
text analysis, 54, 61–65
continuation, Gestalt theory, 70
copyrights
beginner fears, 216
mock-up element, 106
recommendations, 43, 155
Corcoran, Coleen (graphic designer), 14
Creatly (website), 26
credits, source
charts, 43
copyrights, 43, 106, 155, 216
external data, 164
infographics, 23
metadata, 173
cues, visual, 156–158
curb appeal, 166
current state analysis, 91–92, 115–118
customer information, 30–34
cut-off text, 174, 179

• ♪ •

dark backgrounds, 142, 180
Dashboard Insight (website), 195

dashboards, 8, 22, 77. *See also* Business
    Intelligence Dashboard Formula
    (BIDF)
Dashburst (website), 32
data, actionable. *See also* data overload
forecasting, 95
software features, 36
storyboard content, selecting, 86
user impact, 93, 94, 199
data, emotional loss, 193
data, forced to fit aesthetics, 17, 20, 51
data, location
benefits, 159
example, 186
guidelines, 175
use cases, 158–159
Data Informed (website), 176
data overload
clarity, 110–111
example, 183–184
fear of, 218
guidelines, 173
mobile design, 42
One-Shoe-Fits-All Trap, 85, 193–194
text-to-visuals ratio, 61
data visualization(s)
benefits, 2
BI. *See* Business Intelligence (BI)
Big Data, defined, 7, 29–30
City Smart Meter example, evaluation,
    185–186
cluttered example, evaluation, 183–184
cognitive processes, 67–73
definition, 7
design process, 9–10, 73–75
domestic loan example, evaluation,
    176–177
fields of study using, 19–21
food and beverage example, evaluation,
    189–190
high-finance example, evaluation, 180–181
importance, 1, 8
infographics, 13–16, 22–27, 210
insurance policy example, evaluation,
    182–183

data visualization(s) *(continued)*
  mandatory elements, 149–153
  mobile design. *See* mobile design
  mobility survey example, evaluation,
    177–178
  power, 171
  quality indications, 9–11, 34–35, 154
  regional subsidies example, evaluation,
    187–188
  resources, 209–212
  retail dashboard example, evaluation,
    181–182
  Sailboats dashboard example, evaluation,
    188–189
  sales by geography example, evaluation,
    186–187
  SalesForce example, evaluation,
    178–179
  types, defined, 16–17
  users and usage. *See* users and usage
Data Visualization For Dummies Web
    Extras (website), 3
data viz. *See* data visualization
Data-Ink (website), 195
Datavisualization.ch (website), 211
#dataviz Twitter hashtag, 212
delivery speed, 167
demographics, 19, 159
dependability
  data quality, dependence on, 34
  importance, 166
  indications, quality, 9–11, 34–35, 154
  timestamp as indication, 154
  user adoption, 164
description labels, 57
design, mobile content
  benefits, 132–133
  data overload, 42
  device-independent accessibility, 166
  example, 186–187
  guidelines, 175
  intuitive interfaces, 166, 196
  mobile-first mindset, 195–197
  responsive design principles, 76–77
  visual appeal, 131

design principles
  black-and-white mock-ups, 101
  company branding, 139–142
  compromises, 190
  evaluation, 173–175
  humanization, 132–133
  infographics, 23
  interface importance, 131, 166, 196
  "less is more," 75
  navigation, 134–136
  text, 55–56
  web, 59–60
design process
  basics, 9–10
  patterns, 73
  templates, 74–75
Design Your Way (website), 110
Designing Data Visualizations (Iliinsky and
    Steele), 14
desirability, defined, 9
desktop software tools, 103–105
development speed, 167
deviation graphs, 201–202
diagonal text, 57
diagrams, defined, 16
Diamond, Stephanie (author)
  Data Visualization For Dummies, 26
disagreements, 215
Doug Hay & Associates (website), 73
drop-down menus, 137
duplication, avoiding, 174
dynamic cues, 158
dynamic text, 56, 61–63

• E •

ease of use (EOU), 166
easel.ly (website), 26
Education Closet (website), 23
Edward Tufte (website), 209
elements, visual
  correlations, clarity, 111
  device compatibility, 196
  footers, 148, 155, 156
  headers, 148, 152
  help menus, 106

horizontal tab sets, 138
icons, 139, 151, 153, 174
labels, 42, 43, 56–60, 174
links, 147–153
logos, 106
menu selectors, 134, 136–138
menus, guidelines, 77, 132, 175, 196
overlapping, 174
placement patterns, 71–74
templates, 16, 74–75, 105–107
text, 55–61, 174
titles, 57, 106, 164–165
vertical tab sets, 138
visual cues, 156–158
emotional loss of data, 193
entertainment infographics, 26
EOU (ease of use), 166
erasers, 102
evaluation
design, 173–175
design tools, 35–36
worksheet, 172
evaluation examples
City Smart Meter, 185–186
cluttered, 183–184
domestic loan, 176–177
food and beverage, 189–190
high-finance, 180–181
insurance policy, 182–183
mobility survey, 177–178
regional subsidies, 187–188
retail dashboard, 181–182
Sailboats dashboard, 188–189
sales by geography, 186–187
SalesForce, 178–179
Evelson, Bob (author)
"Advanced Data Visualization (ADV)
Platforms," 35
Exact Software (website), 203
Excel (Microsoft)
alternatives to, 49
Excel Charts Blog (website), 211
ineffectiveness, 82
overuse, 191, 192
structured data, 33
Excel Charts Blog (website), 211

exceptions, data points, 112–113,
121–122
executives, mock-ups for, 84, 101
expert advice infographics, 24
Extreme Presentation (website), 217

● *F* ●

F patterns, 72–73
FAQ (Frequently Asked Questions),
152–153
figure/ground, Gestalt theory, 71
filtering, 175
financial sector
charts, 49–51
data visualization, 19–20
geographic data, 159
RAG color use in, 61
flexibility, mobile design, 197
flexible images, 76
flow charts, defined, 17
Flowing Data (website), 211
fluid grids, 76
focus groups. *See also* humanization; user
adoption (UA); users and usage
attention spans, 81, 84, 94, 166–167
colors, mock-ups, 99, 100, 199
common actions, 134
communication, 215
conducting, 89–90
emotional loss of data, 193
executives, 84, 101
goals, 84, 87–89
KPI identification, 90–91
super users, 89, 152, 192
types, 85–86
user engagement, 204–205
fonts
brand standards, 130–140
browser-safe, 59–60
color, 60–61
size, 59
usage guidelines, 174
foot traffic, 158
footers, 148, 155, 156

forcing data to fit aesthetics, 17, 20, 51
forecasting
  calculations, 202–203
  humanization, 126–127
  incorporation into current state
    visuals, 126
  storyboards, 94–95
foreground, Gestalt theory, 71
formatting, conditional
  exceptions, 112–113
  sparing use, 186
  text analysis statements, 62
  visual cues, 157–158
formatting, RAG (red, amber, green) colors
  connotation, 56, 74, 144–145, 158, 217
  financial sector use, 61
  green, misuse, 197–199
  lending clarity, example, 182
  misleading, example, 177
Four Vs of Big Data, 32
Frequently Asked Questions (FAQ),
    152–153
The Functional Art (website), 210
functionality, determining, 133–134

• G •

gauges, 47–48
GE (General Electric) Data Visualization
    (website), 211
generation methods, 14
geographic data
  benefits, 159
  example, 186
  guidelines, 175
  use cases, 158–159
Gestalt theory, 67–71
goal gathering, 84, 87–89
government, 19, 164
graphs, defined, 16
green
  alert connotation, 56, 144–145, 158, 177,
    182, 217
  misleading use, 197–199
grids, importance, 175

ground, Gestalt theory, 71
The Guardian (website), 20
guidelines, design
  black-and-white mock-ups, 101
  company branding, 139–142
  compromises, 190
  evaluation, 173–175
  humanization, 132–133
  infographics, 23
  interface importance, 131, 166, 196
  "less is more," 75
  navigation, 134–136
  text, 55–56
  web, 59–60

• H •

Harvard Business Review, 34
Harvard Business Review Visualizing Data
    (website), 210
hashtags, 212
headers, 148, 152
heat maps, visual patterns, 72–73
help menus, 106
hierarchy, 59, 74
hindsight, defined, 113
historical data, 20–21, 48, 113
hoarding, 192
Home link, 149
horizontal tab sets, 138
horizontal text, 57
Howson, Cindi (founder, BIScorecard), 161
how-to infographics, 25
humanization
  example, 185
  mobile design, 132–133
  phrases, encouraging, 126–127
  techniques, 132
  user interfaces, 131
hypothetical scenarios
  benefits, 175
  BIDF, compared to traditional BI, 90
  mock-ups, 127–129
  storyboards, 95–97

• I •

icons
  FAQ, 153
  guidelines, 174
  navigational, 139
  social media, Share links, 151
icons in book, explained, 2–3
Iliinsky, Noah (author)
  Designing Data Visualizations, 14
images, flexible, 76, 175
immediacy, 11, 18
impact, 121
Indicee (website), 161
indoor mapping, 158
infographics
  data visualizations, compared to, 13–16
  guidelines, 23
  online tools, 26–27
  types, 23–26
  Visual.ly database, 210
Information Builders (website), 185
information technology (IT)
    departments, 194
Infragistics (website), 48, 182
insight, defined, 113
Intel (website), 27
intelligent data. *See also* data overload
  forecasting, 95
  software features, 36
  storyboard content, selecting, 86
  user impact, 93, 94, 199
interactivity
  benefits, 18–19
  data visualizations, compared to
      infographics, 15
  guidelines, 175
  maps, 159
  sliders, example, 176
  tool evaluation, 35
interface, user (UI)
  appearance, importance of, 166
  design standards, 76–77

intuitive, necessity for, 131
  mock-ups, 101
  navigation guidelines, 134–135
internal company data, 164
internal publicity, 166
intuitive design, 196
IT (information technology)
    departments, 194

• J •

job roles, tailoring data for, 86

• K •

Katherine S. Rowell (website), 202
Key Performance Indicators (KPIs)
  on dashboards, 22
  definition, 89
  identification, using scoping
      workshops, 89–91
  mock-ups, 115–118, 121–125, 128
  recommended count, 84
  relative to time, 92
  what-if scenarios, 95–97
  wrong, fear of choosing, 214

• L •

labels
  charts, 42, 43, 58
  color consistency, 60
  as context, 56–57
  guidelines, 174
  hierarchical, 59
landscape orientation, printing, 150–151
last updated timestamp, 154
lawsuits, 155
layout. *See also* mock-ups
  guidelines, 174
  link placement, 147–148
  patterns, 71–74
  templates, 16, 74–75, 105–107

legal matters
  copyright, 43, 106, 155
  fears, 216
  terms and conditions, 156
"less is more" principle, 75
line charts, 44
line of business (LOB), 85
linear scenarios, 200–201
links
  FAQ, 152–153
  Home, 149
  More information, 152
  placement, 147–148
  Print, 150–151
  Reset, 149–150
  Share, 151
  terms and conditions, 156
  usefulness, 77
list boxes, 137
Lloyd, Natasha (graphic-design
    expert), 9
LOB (line of business), 85
location intelligence
  benefits, 159
  example, 186
  guidelines, 175
  use cases, 158–159
Logo Design Love (website), 141
logos, placement, 106
loss prevention, 103

• *M* •

Making Data Meaningful
    (website), 183
maps
  benefits, 159
  example, 186
  guidelines, 175
  use cases, 158–159
Marcia Connor (website), 29
Marcotte, Ethan (author)
  "Responsive Web Design," 76
marketing
  boosting user adoption, 163–167
  demographic data, 159
  split testing, 55

Marketing Message Mindset (website), 26
marketing-campaign performance
  mock-ups, 121, 123–125
  storyboards, 93, 94, 96
Mashable (website), 23, 77
measurements. *See also* Key Performance
    Indicators (KPIs)
  actionable, 93
  identification, using scoping workshops,
    89–91
  monitoring, 47–48
  recommended count, 84
  user adoption, 162–163
  wrong, fear of choosing, 214
media queries, 76–77
Medina, John (author)
  Brain Rules, 17
menus
  design standards, 77, 132, 196
  guidelines, 175
  help, 106
  selectors, 134, 136–138
metadata, 173, 179
metaphors, defined, 17
Metric Insights (website), 113
metrics. *See also* Key Performance
    Indicators (KPIs)
  actionable, 93
  identification, using scoping workshops,
    89–91
  monitoring, 47–48
  recommended count, 84
  user adoption, 162–163
  wrong, fear of choosing, 214
MGM Technology Partners Blog
    (website), 180
Microsoft Excel
  alternatives to, 49
  Excel Charts Blog (website), 211
  ineffectiveness, 82
  overuse, 191, 192
  structured data, 33
mind maps, defined, 17
MindMeister software (website), 17
mistakes, newbie
  chart selection, 49
  color choices, 60, 139, 180

data overload, 93, 192–193
display of unnecessary data, 93
focus group management, 99
green, misuse as alert color, 197–199. *See also* RAG (red, amber, green) colors
inaccurate what-if recommendations, 129
mobile design, neglected, 195–197
One-Shoe-Fits-All Trap, 85, 193–194
pie-chart overuse, 197
statistics, lack of familiarity, 200–203
tool dependence, 194
user engagement, lack of mastery, 204–205
visualization as afterthought, 191
mobile design
benefits, 132–133
data overload, 42
device-independent accessibility, 166
example, 186–187
guidelines, 175
intuitive interfaces, 166, 196
mobile-first mindset, 195–197
responsive design principles, 76–77
visual appeal, 131
mobile devices, data collection, 34
Mockup Tiger (website), evaluation, 104–105
mock-ups. *See also* layout; visual(s)
BIDF BI Blueprint, 115–118, 121–125, 128
color, 100–101
definition, 99
elements, 105–107
executive audiences, 84, 101
hypothetical scenarios, 127–129
importance, 100
pencil and paper, 101–103
software tools, 103–105
More information link, 152

• N •

names, catchy, 164–165
navigation
guidelines, 77, 132, 134–136, 175, 196
help menus, 106
icons, 139
menu selectors, 134, 136–138
navigation area, elements and layout, 106
networking, social
marketing methods, 165
native capability, 197
Share links, 151
Twitter hashtags, 212
Yammer, 165
newbie(s)
color choices, safe, 56, 139–145
fears, 71, 213–218
pencil and paper, advantages, 102
newbie mistakes
chart selection, 49
color choices, 60, 139, 180
data overload, 93, 192–193
display of unnecessary data, 93
focus group management, 99
green, misuse as alert color, 197–199. *See also* RAG (red, amber, green) colors
inaccurate what-if recommendations, 129
mobile design, neglected, 195–197
One-Shoe-Fits-All Trap, 85, 193–194
pie-chart overuse, 197
statistics, lack of familiarity, 200–203
tool dependence, 194
user engagement, lack of mastery, 204–205
visualization as afterthought, 191
Next Generation Food, 165
nonhorizontal text, 57
nonquantifiability, 87, 88

• O •

One-Shoe-Fits-All Trap, 85, 193–194
Online Chart Tool (website), 49
online tools
charts, 49
infographics, 26–27
mock-ups, 103–105
Otus Analytics (website), 48
outliers, 112–113, 121–122

overload, data
  clarity, 110–111
  example, 183–184
  fear of, 218
  guidelines, 173
  mobile design, 42
  One-Shoe-Fits-All Trap, 85, 193–194
  text-to-visuals ratio, 61

• *P* •

Pachal, Pete (author)
  "Apple's 6 Simple Rules for Designing a
    Killer iOS App," 77
pain points, 87
patterns
  design guidelines, 73–74
  F, 72–73
  interactivity benefits, 18
  trend analysis, 18, 121–122
  visual, 71
  Z, 72, 106, 124, 136
Peltier Tech (website), 201
pencil and paper, 101–103
perception, visual, 67–71
performance indicators
  on dashboards, 22
  definition, 89
  identification, using scoping workshops,
    89–91
  mock-ups, 115–118, 121–125, 128
  recommended count, 84
  relative to time, 92
  what-if scenarios, 95–97
  wrong, fear of choosing, 214
personalization
  driving user adoption, example, 189
  guidelines, 174
  interactivity, 18
  photos, example, 185
  tool evaluation, 36
pie charts
  controversy, 44, 197
  limitations, 112
  misuse, 45–47
Piktochart (website), 26, 75
pitfalls, newbie
  chart selection, 49
  color choices, 60, 139, 180

data overload, 93, 192–193
display of unnecessary data, 93
focus group management, 99
green, misuse as alert color, 197–199.
    See also RAG (red, amber, green)
    colors
inaccurate what-if recommendations, 129
mobile design, neglected, 195–197
One-Shoe-Fits-All Trap, 85, 193–194
pie-chart overuse, 197
statistics, lack of familiarity, 200–203
tool dependence, 194
user engagement, lack of mastery,
    204–205
visualization as afterthought, 191
planning, mock-ups. *See also* layout;
    visual(s)
  BIDF BI Blueprint, 115–118, 121–125, 128
  color, 100–101
  definition, 99
  elements, 105–107
  executive audiences, 84, 101
  hypothetical scenarios, 127–129
  importance, 100
  pencil and paper, 101–103
  software tools, 103–105
planning, storyboards
  audience, 85–91
  building process, 91–97
  Current State section, 91–92
  Forecast section, 94–95
  goal-gathering process, 87–89
  KPI identification, 89–91
  preliminary steps, 84
  sections, 83
  Trends section, 92–94
  What-if section, 95–97
  wrong stories, fear of telling, 213–214
Playfair, William (engineer)
  pie chart invention, 47
  The Statistical Breviary, 101
politics, data use, 19
portrait orientation, printing, 150–151
predictive analysis and forecasting
  calculations, 202–203
  humanization, 126–127
  incorporation into current state
    visuals, 126
  storyboards, 94–95

Prichard, Joe (graphic designer), 14
principles, design
  black-and-white mock-ups, 101
  company branding, 139–142
  compromises, 190
  evaluation, 173–175
  humanization, 132–133
  infographics, 23
  interface importance, 131, 166, 196
  "less is more," 75
  navigation, 134–136
  text, 55–56
  web, 59–60
Print link, 150–151
printing, orientation, 150–151
probabilty, 200–201
process, design
  basics, 9–10
  patterns, 73
  templates, 74–75
proof of concept, 167
prototypes. *See also* visuals
  BIDF BI Blueprint, 115–118, 121–125, 128
  color, 100–101
  definition, 99
  elements, 105–107
  executive audiences, 84, 101
  hypothetical scenarios, 127–129
  importance, 100
  pencil and paper, 101–103
  software tools, 103–105
proximity, Gestalt theory, 68–69
publicity
  boosting user adoption, 163–167
  demographic data, 159
  split testing, 55

• Q •

QlikView (website), 37, 178
quality
  indications, 9–11, 34–35, 154
  priorities, 77, 197, 214
quantifiability, 87, 88

• R •

radar charts, 49–51
radio buttons, 138
RAG (red, amber, green) colors
  alert connotation, 56, 74, 144–145, 158, 217
  financial sector use, 61
  green, misuse, 197–199
  lending clarity, example, 182
  misleading, example, 177
RD (responsive design), 76–77, 175. *See also* mobile design
Recovery.gov (website), 19
regression modeling, 87
reliability
  data quality, dependence on, 34
  importance, 166
  indications, quality, 9–11, 34–35, 154
  timestamp as indication, 154
  user adoption, 164
Remember icon, explained, 2
repetition, in pattern design, 74
Reset link, 149–150
resources, 209–212
Resources Research (website), 119
responsive design (RD), 76–77, 175. *See also* mobile design
"Responsive Web Design" (Marcotte), 76
retail, 158
Rich Chart Live (website), 49
risk level, what-ifs, 96

• S •

Salesforce Chatter, 165
Salt Mountains visualization, 165
SAP Dashboard Gallery (website), 177
scalability, of system, 10
scenarios, what-if
  benefits, 175
  BIDF, compared to traditional BI, 90
  mock-ups, 127–129
  storyboards, 95–97
science, data use, 20

scoping workshops. *See also* humanization;
    user adoption (UA); users and usage
  attention spans, 81, 84, 94, 166–167
  colors, mock-ups, 99, 100, 199
  common actions, 134
  communication, 215
  conducting, 89–90
  definition, 89
  emotional loss of data, 193
  executives, 84, 101
  goals, 84, 87–89
  KPI identification, 89–91, 90–91
  super users, 89, 152, 192
  types, 85–86
  user engagement, 204–205
scorecards, 48, 112
Search Engine Land (website), 76
search engines, 76–77
security, against loss, 103
seeing
  patterns, 71–73
  perception, 67–71
  visual cues, 156–158
Share link, 151
SignageLive (website), 198
similarity, Gestalt theory, 69
simplicity
  app design, 77
  charts, 42
  guidelines, 173
  interactivity, 18
  mobile design, 133
  text, 55–56
SmartDraw (website), 44
smartphones, content design
  benefits, 132–133
  data overload, 42
  device-independent accessibility, 166
  example, 186–187
  guidelines, 175
  mobile-first mindset, 195–197
  responsive design principles, 76–77
  visual appeal, 131
smartphones, data collection, 34
social economics, data use, 19–20
social media
  marketing methods, 165
  native capability, 197

Share links, 151
Twitter hashtags, 212
Yammer, 165
software
  charts, 49
  Exact Software, 203
  infographics, 26–27
  Microsoft Excel, 33, 82, 191,
    192, 211
  MindMeister, 17
  mock-up tools, 103–105
  Piktochart (website), 26, 75
  QlikView, 37
  Tableau, 36–37, 187
source credits
  charts, 43
  copyrights, 43, 106, 155, 216
  external data, 164
  infographics, 23
  metadata, 173
speed, 166–167
split testing, 55
Stack (website), 25
stakeholders
  attention spans, 81, 84, 94, 166–167
  colors, mock-ups, 99, 100, 199
  common actions, 134
  communication, 215
  emotional loss of data, 193
  executives, 84, 101
  goals, 84, 87–89
  KPIs, 89–91
  super users, 89, 152, 192
  types, 85–86
  user engagement, 204–205
static visualizations, 15–16
statistics, 200–203
Steele, Julia (author)
  Designing Data Visualizations, 14
Stikeleather, Jim (author)
  "When Data Visualization Works – and
    When It Doesn't," 34
stock markets, 49–50
storyboards
  audience, 85–91
  building process, 91–97
  Current State section, 91–92
  Forecast section, 94–95

goal-gathering process, 87–89
KPI identification, 89–91
preliminary steps, 84
sections, 83
Trends section, 92–94
What-if section, 95–97
wrong stories, fear of telling, 213–214
structured data, 33
success, business techniques, 194, 204–205
super users, 89, 152, 192
system scalability, 10

● *T* ●

tab sets, 138
Tableau Software (website), 36–37, 187
tables, 112, 174
tablets, content design
benefits, 132–133
data overload, 42
device-independent accessibility, 166
example, 186–187
guidelines, 175
mobile-first mindset, 195–197
responsive design principles, 76–77
visual appeal, 131
tablets, data collection, 34
teamwork. *See also* focus groups; social
media
design tools, 102–103
disagreements, 215
impact on user adoption, 161
interactivity benefits, 18
link sharing, 151
mobile design, 133, 197
mock-ups, 103
Technical Stuff icon, explained, 3
templates
benefits, 74–75
creation, 105–107
definition, 16
terms and conditions, 156, 216
text
color, 60–61
cut-off, 174, 179
dynamic, 56, 61–63
fonts, 58–60

guidelines, 55–56, 174
hierarchies, 59
labels, 56–57
positioning, 57–58
text analysis, 54, 61–65
text-to-visuals ratio, 61
The Statistical Breviary (Playfair), 101
*The Visual Display of Quantitative
Information* (Tufte), 45
3-D, 42
time, relativity, 92
timelines, 16, 23, 24
timestamps, 154
Tip icon, explained, 2
titles
catchy, 164–165
description, 57
mock-ups, 106
T-models, 87
tools
beginner fears, 216
dependence, 194
evaluation and choice, 35–36
mock-ups, 103–105
online, 26–27, 49
pencil and paper, 101–103
wrong, fear of choosing, 216–217
training, 166
transportation data, 158
trend analysis
marketing campaign performance,
123–125
patterns, 18, 121–122
representation techniques, 119–120
storyboards, 92–94
trustworthiness
data quality, dependence on, 34
importance, 166
indications, quality, 9–11, 34–35, 154
timestamp as indication, 154
user adoption, 164
Tufte, Edward (author)
*The Visual Display of Quantitative
Information,* 45, 110
website, 209
24/7 availability, 166
Twitter hashtags, 212

typefaces
  brand standards, 130–140
  browser-safe, 59–60
  color, 60–61
  size, 59
  usage guidelines, 174

• *U* •

UA (user adoption)
  accessibility, 11, 166
  barriers, 161
  marketing techniques,
    163–167
  measurements, 162–163
  overview, 162
  personalization, 189
UI (user interface)
  appearance, importance
    of, 166
  design standards, 76–77
  intuitive, necessity for, 131
  mock-ups, 101
  navigation guidelines, 134–135
understandability, 22–23
unstructured data, 33–34
updates
  dashboards, 22
  timestamps, 154
  user adoption measurements, 162
usability, 9, 11
usefulness, defined, 9
user adoption (UA)
  accessibility, 11, 166
  barriers, 161–162
  marketing techniques, 163–167
  measurements, 162–163
  overview, 162
  personalization, 189
user interface (UI)
  appearance, importance of, 166
  design standards, 76–77
  intuitive, necessity for, 131, 196
  mock-ups, 101
  navigation guidelines, 134–135

users and usage
  actions, 133–134
  alert colors. *See* RAG (red, amber, green)
    colors
  attention spans, 81, 84, 94, 166–167
  audience types, 8, 85–86
  common actions, 134
  dashboards, 22
  emotional loss, 193
  engagement, 204–205
  executives, 101
  filters, 175
  finance and social economics, 19–20
  goals, 87–89
  history, 20–21
  humanization. *See* humanization
  IT department approval, 194
  KPIs, 89–91
  politics and government, 19
  user adoption. *See* user adoption (UA)
  visual behavior, 67–73

• *V* •

value. *See also* data overload
  aesthetics, less important than data,
    23, 214
  Big Data brings to business, 30–31
  charts, valueless, 49–50, 217
  color, 42, 173
  determined by data quality,
    34–35, 154
  exceptions to trends, 113
  impact of visuals, 121
  statistical insight, 200–203
  traits, 9
  user adoption, as measure, 162–164
value labels (numerical), 57
variance, 201–202
variety, defined, 32
velocity, defined, 32
Venngage (website), 26
veracity, defined, 32
vertical tab sets, 138
vertical text, 57

Visifire (website), 50
visual(s). *See also* color
  cues, 156–158
  current state KPIs, 115–118
  effectiveness, 110–113
  forecasts, 125–127
  impact, 121
  initial creation process, 115–129
  links, 149–153
  metrics observations, during creation
      process, 116–118, 122, 124
  patterns, 71–73
  perception, 67–71
  querying, defined, 35
  timestamps, 154
  trend analysis, 118–125
  what-ifs, 127–129
visual appeal
  data visualizations, compared to
      infographics, 14
  importance, 10, 166
  mobile design, importance to, 131
  ugly visualizations, fear of, 214
  valueless without effective data, 109
  white space, 74, 142, 173, 180–181, 195
  worthless without information, 23
*The Visual Display of Quantitative
    Information* (Tufte), 45, 110
visual elements
  correlations, clarity, 111
  device compatibility, 196
  footers, 148, 155, 156
  headers, 148, 152
  help menus, 106
  horizontal tab sets, 138
  icons, 139, 151, 153, 174
  labels, 42, 43, 56–60, 174
  links, 147–153
  logos, 106
  menu selectors, 134, 136–138
  menus, guidelines, 77, 132,
      175, 196
  overlapping, 174
  placement patterns, 71–74
  templates, 16, 74–75, 105–107
  text, 55–61, 174

titles, 57, 106, 164–165
vertical tab sets, 138
visual cues, 156–158
visualizations, data
  benefits, 2
  BI. *See* Business Intelligence (BI)
  Big Data, defined, 7, 29–30
  City Smart Meter example, evaluation,
      185–186
  cluttered example, evaluation, 183–184
  cognitive processes, 67–73
  definition, 7
  design process, 9–10, 73–75
  domestic loan example, evaluation,
      176–177
  fields of study using, 19–21
  food and beverage example, evaluation,
      189–190
  high-finance example, evaluation,
      180–181
  importance, 1, 8
  infographics, 13–16, 22–27, 210
  insurance policy example, evaluation,
      182–183
  mandatory elements, 149–153
  mobile design. *See* mobile design
  mobility survey example, evaluation,
      177–178
  power, 171
  quality indications, 9–11, 10–11,
      34–35, 154
  regional subsidies example, evaluation,
      187–188
  resources, 209–212
  retail dashboard example, evaluation,
      181–182
  Sailboats dashboard example, evaluation,
      188–189
  sales by geography example, evaluation,
      186–187
  SalesForce example, evaluation, 178–179
  types, defined, 16–17
  users and usage. *See* users and usage
Visualizing Data (website), 210
Visual.ly (website), 21, 127, 210
volume, defined, 32

• W •

warning colors, RAG (red, amber, green)
  connotation, 56, 74, 144–145, 158, 217
  financial sector use, 61
  green, misuse, 197–199
  lending clarity, example, 182
  misleading, example, 177
Warning icon, explained, 3
warnings, visualizing
  dashboards, 22
  exceptions, 112–113
  green, misleading use of, 197–199
  red, misleading use of, 74
  sparing use, 186
  stakeholder notifications, 36
  text analysis statements, 62
  visual cues, 157–158
waterfall charts, 49–51
web design, 59–60. *See also* mobile design
Web Extras (website), 3, 90
web-based software
  charts, 49
  infographics, 26–27
  mock-ups, 103–105
What About Me? online infographic tool, 27
What your coffee says about you
    infographic (website), 15
what-if scenarios
  benefits, 175
  BIDF, compared to traditional BI, 90
  mock-ups, 127–129
  storyboards, 95–97
white and black, for mock-ups, 100–101
white space
  examples, 178, 180, 181, 195
  guidelines, 173
  importance, 142
  pattern design, 74
Wikimedia (website), 140

wireframes. *See also* visuals
  BIDF BI Blueprint, 115–118, 121–125, 128
  color, 100–101
  definition, 99
  elements, 105–107
  executive audiences, 84, 101
  hypothetical scenarios, 127–129
  importance, 100
  pencil and paper, 101–103
  software tools, 103–105
word clouds, 26
Wordle (website), 26
word-of-mouth, 164
words and text
  color, 60–61
  cut-off, 174, 179
  dynamic, 56, 61–63
  fonts, 58–60
  guidelines, 55–56, 174
  hierarchies, 59
  labels, 56–57
  positioning, 57–58
WTF Viz (website), 111

• Y •

Yammer (website), 165
Yau, Nathan (data visualist), 211
yellow
  "caution" connotation, 56, 61, 145, 217
  contrast, need for, 116
Yuhanna, Noel (author)
  "Advanced Data Visualization (ADV)
    Platforms," 35
Yuk, Mico (author)
  Data Visualization For Dummies, 9

• Z •

Z patterns, 72, 136

About the Authors

Mico Yuk is a thought leader in business analytics and business intelligence (BI). She has more than 8 years of experience working with Fortune 200 companies around the globe to help them develop cutting-edge decision-making visual and reporting tools. By 2012 she was rated number 13 on SAP's list of the 50 top analytics influencers in the industry. As a number-one rated global speaker, blogger, and business intelligence coach, she has trained thousands of students using her "tell like it is" style of teaching.

Mico started out as BI consultant working on major initiatives with companies such as LG Electronics, Pfizer, Allstate Insurance, Bank of America, VISA MasterCard, Qatargas, Conoco Phillips, and many more.

In 2008 she founded a blog named EverythingXcelsius.com (http://everythingxcelsius.com) and the Xcelsius Gurus Network to bring the BusinessObjects community together after the SAP acquisition. Within a year it became a number-one blog within the SAP Business Intelligence ecosystem. In 2012 and 2013 she founded the BI Dashboard Formula program and the BI Brainz group to focus on the "soft side" of business intelligence. Her training and programs drew in almost 1,000 students online. During its six-country tour in 2013, it quickly became one of the top BI programs in the industry with success stories from companies like Nestle, Shell, and SAP Power Networks.

Mico received a BS in Computer Engineering with a minor in Mathematics from the University of Miami (Florida). Born and raised on the beautiful island of St. Croix, she resides in Atlanta, Georgia where she enjoys spending time with family, working out, and finding time to be next to the ocean whenever possible.

Stephanie Diamond is a thought leader and management marketing professional with 20+ years of experience building profits in more than 75 different industries. She has worked with solo-preneurs, small business owners, and multibillion dollar corporations. As a best-selling author she has written a total of seven business books including, *Social Media Marketing For Dummies* and *The Visual Marketing Revolution*.

She worked for eight years as a Marketing Director at AOL. When she joined the company, there were fewer than 1 million subscribers. When Stephanie left AOL in 2002, there were 36 million subscribers. While at AOL, she developed a highly successful line of multimedia products that brought in an annual $40 million in incremental revenue.

In 2002 Stephanie founded Digital Media Works, Inc. (MarketingMessageMindset.com) an online marketing company that helps business owners discover the hidden profits in their businesses. She is passionate about guiding online companies to successfully generate more revenue and find their company's real value.

As a strategic thinker, Stephanie uses all the current visual thinking techniques and brain research to help companies get to the essence of their brands. She continues to focus on helping companies understand and communicate their value to customers.

Stephanie received a BA in Psychology from Hofstra University and an MSW and MPH from the University of Hawaii. She lives in New York with her husband. They have a Maltese named Colby.

Dedication

To my family — mother Nadina, sisters Soo and Anna, aunt Tamica, and niece Cabria — who always support my crazy ideas, and tendency to jump in head first!

To my late high school art teacher, Anselm Richards, for being crazy enough to think I could be an artist. You would have loved to see what all those art classes turned into.

To my industry mentors — Lewis Temares, Rick Montgomery, and Cliff Alper — for seeing potential in me and taking the time to nurture it.

To Will Johnson, the best manager ever, who allowed me to be creative and learn on company time!

To my best friend Ryan Goodman for his unparalleled support, like-minded passion, and a high tolerance for crazy.

To all of my BIDF students who continue to push me and influence me on a daily basis. Thanks for believing in the vision and the methodology every day.

— *Mico Yuk*

To Barry, who makes all things possible.

To my family, for their encouragement and love.

— *Stephanie Diamond*

Author's Acknowledgments

It's an honor to write about something that I'm so passionate about: data visualization. A big thank you to John Wiley & Sons, Inc. for providing me the opportunity to share my experiences with the world.

The following list of people I owe a sincere thanks for their influence, enthusiasm, and ability to make me think outside the box for this book.

- To the insanely patient group at Wiley — Senior Acquisitions Editor Katie Mohr and Project Editor Charlotte Kughen — for working around my crazy schedule and helping me to pursue this dream.
- To my top BIDF students: Ron Reago and Lee Taylor (Shell Oil), Matt Grygorcewicz from (SAP Power Networks), and John Boughflower (Royal Mail). You continuously challenged me and proved our methodology is a game-changer!
- To Stephanie Diamond for dedication in co-authoring this book.

— *Mico Yuk*

It is my great privilege to write a book on data visualization. I want to offer great thanks to John Wiley Publishing, Inc. for letting me present my ideas about why data visualization is an important concept that will influence businesses for a long time to come.

The following people were especially important in creating this book, and I offer very sincere thanks:

- To the magnificent and clever group at Wiley, Senior Acquisitions Editor Katie Mohr, Project Editor Charlotte Kughen, Tech Editor Andrew Moore, and Copy Editor Kathy Simpson.
- To Matt Wagner, my agent at Fresh Books, for his continued hard work on my behalf.
- To Mico Yuk for sharing her great knowledge co-authoring this book.
- To the talented and wise thought leaders named in this book who influence my ideas about data visualization.

Finally, to the smart readers who will take this book far beyond the goals we had. Enjoy the data visualization journey!

— *Stephanie Diamond*

Publisher's Acknowledgments

Senior Acquisitions Editor: Katie Mohr

Project Editor: Charlotte Kughen

Copy Editor: Kathy Simpson

Technical Editor: Andrew Moore

Editorial Assistant: Anne Sullivan

Sr. Editorial Assistant: Cherie Case

Project Coordinator: Sheree Montgomery

Cover Image: Analysis Factory (front cover),
BI Brainz (back cover)

ple & Mac

ad For Dummies,
h Edition
8-1-118-49823-1

hone 5 For Dummies,
h Edition
8-1-118-35201-4

acBook For Dummies,
h Edition
8-1-118-20920-2

S X Mountain Lion
r Dummies
8-1-118-39418-2

logging & Social Media

acebook For Dummies,
h Edition
8-1-118-09562-1

om Blogging
r Dummies
8-1-118-03843-7

interest For Dummies
8-1-118-32800-2

ordPress For Dummies,
h Edition
8-1-118-38318-6

usiness

ommodities For Dummies,
nd Edition
8-1-118-01687-9

vesting For Dummies,
h Edition
8-0-470-90545-6

Personal Finance
For Dummies,
7th Edition
978-1-118-11785-9

QuickBooks 2013
For Dummies
978-1-118-35641-8

Small Business Marketing Kit
For Dummies,
3rd Edition
978-1-118-31183-7

Careers

Job Interviews
For Dummies,
4th Edition
978-1-118-11290-8

Job Searching with
Social Media
For Dummies
978-0-470-93072-4

Personal Branding
For Dummies
978-1-118-11792-7

Resumes For Dummies,
6th Edition
978-0-470-87361-8

Success as a Mediator
For Dummies
978-1-118-07862-4

Diet & Nutrition

Belly Fat Diet For Dummies
978-1-118-34585-6

Eating Clean For Dummies
978-1-118-00013-7

Nutrition For Dummies,
5th Edition
978-0-470-93231-5

Digital Photography

Digital Photography
For Dummies,
7th Edition
978-1-118-09203-3

Digital SLR Cameras &
Photography For Dummies,
4th Edition
978-1-118-14489-3

Photoshop Elements 11
For Dummies
978-1-118-40821-6

Gardening

Herb Gardening
For Dummies,
2nd Edition
978-0-470-61778-6

Vegetable Gardening
For Dummies,
2nd Edition
978-0-470-49870-5

Health

Anti-Inflammation Diet
For Dummies
978-1-118-02381-5

Diabetes For Dummies,
3rd Edition
978-0-470-27086-8

Living Paleo For Dummies
978-1-118-29405-5

Hobbies

Beekeeping
For Dummies
978-0-470-43065-1

eBay For Dummies,
7th Edition
978-1-118-09806-6

Raising Chickens
For Dummies
978-0-470-46544-8

Wine For Dummies,
5th Edition
978-1-118-28872-6

Writing Young Adult Fiction
For Dummies
978-0-470-94954-2

Language & Foreign Language

500 Spanish Verbs
For Dummies
978-1-118-02382-2

English Grammar
For Dummies,
2nd Edition
978-0-470-54664-2

French All-in One
For Dummies
978-1-118-22815-9

German Essentials
For Dummies
978-1-118-18422-6

Italian For Dummies,
2nd Edition
978-1-118-00465-4

Available in print and e-book formats.

Math & Science

Algebra I For Dummies,
2nd Edition
978-0-470-55964-2

Anatomy and Physiology
For Dummies,
2nd Edition
978-0-470-92326-9

Astronomy For Dummies,
3rd Edition
978-1-118-37697-3

Biology For Dummies,
2nd Edition
978-0-470-59875-7

Chemistry For Dummies,
2nd Edition
978-1-1180-0730-3

Pre-Algebra Essentials
For Dummies
978-0-470-61838-7

Microsoft Office

Excel 2013 For Dummies
978-1-118-51012-4

Office 2013 All-in-One
For Dummies
978-1-118-51636-2

PowerPoint 2013
For Dummies
978-1-118-50253-2

Word 2013 For Dummies
978-1-118-49123-2

Music

Blues Harmonica
For Dummies
978-1-118-25269-7

Guitar For Dummies,
3rd Edition
978-1-118-11554-1

iPod & iTunes
For Dummies,
10th Edition
978-1-118-50864-0

Programming

Android Application
Development For
Dummies, 2nd Edition
978-1-118-38710-8

iOS 6 Application
Development For Dummies
978-1-118-50880-0

Java For Dummies,
5th Edition
978-0-470-37173-2

Religion & Inspiration

The Bible For Dummies
978-0-7645-5296-0

Buddhism For Dummies,
2nd Edition
978-1-118-02379-2

Catholicism For Dummies,
2nd Edition
978-1-118-07778-8

Self-Help & Relationships

Bipolar Disorder
For Dummies,
2nd Edition
978-1-118-33882-7

Meditation For Dummies,
3rd Edition
978-1-118-29144-3

Seniors

Computers For Seniors
For Dummies,
3rd Edition
978-1-118-11553-4

iPad For Seniors
For Dummies,
5th Edition
978-1-118-49708-1

Social Security
For Dummies
978-1-118-20573-0

Smartphones & Tablets

Android Phones
For Dummies
978-1-118-16952-0

Kindle Fire HD
For Dummies
978-1-118-42223-6

NOOK HD For Dummies,
Portable Edition
978-1-118-39498-4

Surface For Dummies
978-1-118-49634-3

Test Prep

ACT For Dummies,
5th Edition
978-1-118-01259-8

ASVAB For Dummies,
3rd Edition
978-0-470-63760-9

GRE For Dummies,
7th Edition
978-0-470-88921-3

Officer Candidate Tests,
For Dummies
978-0-470-59876-4

Physician's Assistant Exa
For Dummies
978-1-118-11556-5

Series 7 Exam
For Dummies
978-0-470-09932-2

Windows 8

Windows 8 For Dummies
978-1-118-13461-0

Windows 8 For Dummies,
Book + DVD Bundle
978-1-118-27167-4

Windows 8 All-in-One
For Dummies
978-1-118-11920-4

e **Available in print and e-book formats.**

Take Dummies with you everywhere you go!

Whether you're excited about e-books, want more from the web, must have your mobile apps, or swept up in social media, Dummies makes everything easier .

Visit Us

Like Us

Follow Us

Watch Us

Join Us

Pin Us

Circle Us

Shop Us

Dummies products make life easier

- DIY
- Consumer Electronics
- Crafts
- Software
- Cookware
- Hobbies
- Videos
- Music
- Games
- and More!

For more information, go to **Dummies.com**® and search the store by category.